# I Reach for the Stars

# I Reach for the Stars

*An Autobiography*

Barbara Cartland

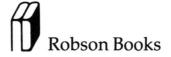

Robson Books

First published in Great Britain in 1994 by Robson Books Ltd, Bolsover House, 5–6 Clipstone Street, London W1P 7EB

**British Library and Cataloguing in Publication Data**
A catalogue record for this title is available from the British Library

ISBN 0 86051 924 4

Set in Palatino by Selwood Systems, Midsomer Norton.
Printed in Great Britain by Butler & Tanner Ltd, Frome and London.

# By Barbara Cartland

*Romantic Novels*, over 500, the most recently published being:

| | |
|---|---|
| *A Miracle for Love* | *Love and the Gods* |
| *A Virgin Bride* | *Love Conquers War* |
| *A Royal Love Match* | *A Sacrifice for Love* |
| *A Steeplechase for Love* | *A Call of Love* |
| *Search for a Wife* | *A Heart Finds Love* |
| *A Shooting Star* | *She Wanted Love* |
| *The Duke Is Deceived* | *A Prayer for Love* |
| *The Queen Wins* | *Wish Upon a Star* |
| *Love and the Clans* | *A Road to Romance* |
| *The Winning Post Is Love* | *Soft, Sweet and Gentle* |

*The Dream and the Glory* (In aid of the St. John Ambulance Brigade)

*Autobiographical and Biographical*

| | |
|---|---|
| *The Isthmus Years* | 1919–39 |
| *The Years of Opportunity* | 1939–45 |
| *I Search for Rainbows* | 1945–76 |
| *We Danced All Night* | 1919–29 |

*Ronald Cartland* (With a foreword by Sir Winston Churchill)
*Polly – My Wonderful Mother*
*I Seek the Miraculous*

*Historical*

*Bewitching Women*
*The Outrageous Queen* (The Story of Queen Christina of Sweden)
*The Scandalous Life of King Carol*
*The Private Life of Charles II*
*The Private Life of Elizabeth, Empress of Austria*
*Josephine, Empress of France*
*Diane de Poitiers*
*Metternich – The Passionate Diplomat*
*A Year of Royal Days*
*Royal Jewels*
*Royal Eccentrics*
*Royal Lovers*

*Sociology*

| | |
|---|---|
| *You in the Home* | *Etiquette* |
| *The Fascinating Forties* | *The Many Facets of Love* |
| *Marriage for Moderns* | *Sex and the Teenager* |
| *Be Vivid, Be Vital* | *The Book of Charm* |
| *Love, Life and Sex* | *Living Together* |
| *Vitamins for Vitality* | *The Youth Secret* |
| *Husbands and Wives* | *The Magic of Honey* |

*Keep Young and Beautiful* by Barbara Cartland and Elinor Glyn
*Etiquette for Love and Romance*
*Barbara Cartland's Book of Health*

*Cookery*

Barbara Cartland's *Health Food Cookery Book*
*Food for Love*
*Magic of Honey Cookbook*
*Recipes for Lovers*
*The Romance of Food*

*Editor of*

*The Common Problem* by Ronald Cartland (with a preface by the
Rt. Hon. The Earl of Selbourne, P.C.
Barbara Cartland's *Library of Love*
*Library of Ancient Wisdom*
*Written with Love* Passionate love letters selected by Barbara
Cartland

*Drama*

*Blood Money*
*French Dressing*

*Philosophy*

*Touch the Stars*

*Radio Operetta*

*The Rose and the Violet* (Music by Mark Lubbock, performed in
1942)

*Radio Play*

*The Caged Bird* An Episode in the life of Elizabeth, Empress of Austria, performed in 1957

*General*

*Barbara Cartland's Book of Useless Information* with a Foreword by the Earl Mountbatten of Burma (In aid of the United World Colleges)
*Love and Lovers* (Picture Book)
*The Light of Love* (Prayer Book)
*Barbara Cartland's Scrapbook* (In aid of the Royal Photographic Museum)
*Romantic Royal Marriages*
*Barbara Cartland's Book of Celebrities*
*Getting Older, Growing Younger*

*Verse*

*Lines on Life and Love*

*Cartoons*

*Barbara Cartland Romances* (Book of Cartoons) has recently been published in the U.S.A., Great Britain, and other parts of the world

*Children*

*Princess to the Rescue* A Children's Pop-Up Book

*Music*

An Album of *Love Songs* sung with the Royal Philharmonic Orchestra

*Films and Videos*

*A Hazard of Hearts*
*The Lady and the Highwayman*
*A Ghost in Monte Carlo*
*A Duel of Hearts*

# Awards

1945 Received Certificate of Merit, Eastern Command, for being Welfare Officer to 5,000 troops in Bedfordshire.

1953 Made a Commander of the Order of St. John of Jerusalem. Invested by H.R.H. The Duke of Gloucester at Buckingham Palace.

1972 Invested as Dame of Grace of the Order of St. John in London by The Lord Prior, Lord Caccia.

1981 Received 'Achiever of the Year' from the National Home Furnishing Association in Colorado Springs, U.S.A. for her designs for wallpaper and fabrics.

1984 Received Bishop Wright Air Industry Award at Kennedy Airport, for inventing the aeroplane-towed glider.

1988 Received from Monsieur Chirac, the Prime Minister of France, the Gold Medal of the City of Paris, for selling 25 million books and giving a lot of employment.

1991 Invested as Dame of the Order of the British Empire, by H.M. The Queen at Buckingham Palace for her contribution to Literature.

# Chapter One

Only the Americans would ask you to write your Obituary before you died.

In 1978 the Americans asked me to do mine and I laughed. I thought it was a joke that they wanted you to write it all down before you passed over.

However, thinking about it I came to the conclusion that it would be very useful to have my own heraldic Family Tree correct and up-to-date.

In the past people had written about me and my daughter and got it entirely wrong. I had always been told that my Mother's family was an old Saxon family from Devonshire starting with the name Scoberhull which eventually changed to Scobell.

However, there seemed to be little written about them until my Great-Uncle Captain Treweeke Scobell proposed the idea of the Victoria Cross for Valour, to be made from the guns which had been used in the battle of the Crimea.

This was received with great enthusiasm. So much so that Captain Scobell was asked to withdraw his motion so that it might be put forward by Queen

Victoria herself. My Great-Uncle agreed to this and stepped aside.

My Grandfather Colonel George Treweeke Scobell was a very unusual character. He was one of the first men to climb Mont Blanc, for which he received a diploma. He was there at the opening of the Suez Canal.

He went round the world in a sailing ship three times and boasted of having made love to a woman of every nationality and thought the Japanese were best.

He and my Grandmother were among the first passengers on the Trans-Siberian Railway.

My Grandfather had five children. Three girls besides my Mother, and one precious boy at the end.

His son, my Uncle, Sir John Scobell, distinguished himself in the Army and was instrumental in laying down the defence of Malta for which he was knighted. He eventually became Governor of the Tower of London.

When my Grandfather married he settled down in a large attractive Victorian house in Redmarley in Gloucestershire.

I remember as a child being impressed by the butler and three footmen who looked after us at meals. Also the large number of servants who came in for the Morning Prayers which took place before breakfast every day.

I was the daughter of my Grandfather's third daughter who was christened Mary but called Polly because she talked so much. She was very small, very attractive with deep brown eyes to match her hair.

She was dancing energetically at a ball when a tall,

handsome young man of twenty-three saw her and said: 'That is the girl I am going to marry.'

His name was James Bertram Falkner Cartland.

He was the only son of a great financier. His Father, James Cartland, had married a Scottish beauty called Flora Falkner and built himself a large house near Birmingham in Warwickshire.

He was instrumental in turning Birmingham, which was then a small city, into a large and important one.

He was offered first a knighthood then twice a baronetcy. He refused them all.

He was very important but my Grandfather opposed the marriage because he was earning his living. In his day a gentleman did not have anything to do with trade.

My Father and Mother however married and were exceedingly happy until disaster struck.

Just after I was born my Grandfather had financed the Fishguard Railway which later was a huge success.

But in 1902 there was a recession just as we have now and the banks called in their loans.

They told my Grandfather he would have to live on his dividends of £6,000 a year with Income Tax at eleven pence in the pound. But because he was not well at the time he felt he could not be poor and therefore shot himself.

There was no limited liability in those days and everything my Grandfather owned was sold.

My Father and Mother had to give up their large and very comfortable house in Worcestershire and move to a smaller house in Pershore called Amerie

Court which was offered to them for £40 a year by a great friend, the famous Earl of Coventry.

I remember it had an enormous garden where I was certain the fairies played in the plum trees. I listened at the trunks of the large trees to hear the goblins.

The house was very comfortable and I had a nanny who was paid £15 a year. There was also a general maid.

My Father and Mother, as they knew everyone in the neighbourhood, went on enjoying parties and shoots.

My Father only kept one horse and they had to bicycle to a great number of places.

I was writing out my biography for America when I thought of my Great-Grandmother after whom I had been called. In fact I was christened Mary Barbara Hamilton.

She had been a great beauty and a rich heiress who had come from Philadelphia to England where she met a Scobell and fell very much in love. She was very tiny but had seven children before she was twenty-seven. Unfortunately she died after giving birth to the last one.

My Grandmother was the sixth and they had always spoken of her as being a very remarkable person.

I also learnt that her Grandfather who became the Governor of Philadelphia was a descendant of the Dukes of Hamilton.

I rang up the present Duke to ask if this was true.

He told me it was. He could not remember who it was but his ancestor had killed someone of great importance in a duel. That was why he had had to flee the country.

Having settled that, I then turned to my Father's antecedents and remembered vaguely that two older cousins had once told me we were related to Robert the Bruce, King of Scotland.

I telephoned the Lord Lyon and told him that my Grandmother had been Flora Falkner and he said at once:

'Yes, King Robert the Bruce had a very large family, and they all kept hawks, but your Grandmother was definitely related to him.'

'Are you saying,' I asked, 'that I can call myself a direct descendant of King Robert the Bruce? Because you know if I am not exactly right about it people will think I am trying to make myself sound important.'

'Then tell them to telephone me,' the Lord Lyon said.

I was delighted at what he had told me. I was very proud to be a Scot.

I found out also from the Lord Lyon that there had been a Cartland Clan in 1220 in Lanarkshire.

They registered their Arms and there was first a village and then a town called after them.

To this day there are the Cartland Craggs, a beauty spot on the River Mole where Scotland's hero Wallace hid from the English. They could not find him although they killed his wife for delaying them.

That was my past history.

After receiving forty-nine proposals of marriage I accepted the fiftieth.

One reason I was very anxious to be married was so that I could have children.

I love children and had as my bridesmaids ten small children all dressed in pink who looked like rose-buds and were greatly admired by everyone who saw them. In fact they were so attractive that the Press gave publicity to one or two of them every day with a photograph.

Alexander McCorquodale, whom I married in April 1927, had great charm. His family lived in a delightful Queen Anne house in Staffordshire with a huge garden. I thought how much my children would love it.

Unfortunately for the first year no baby arrived and I was very worried until finally in the second year of our marriage I had a child.

I had always thought because I had loved my brothers so much that I would want a large family of boys with perhaps just two girls later on.

However the Scots fey in me which has worked all through my life told me instinctively that I was going to have a daughter.

I was determined that if I was she should be beautiful. I had suffered so much myself by hearing people say I was plain when I was young.

I had therefore prayed every night that I would be beautiful as I thought my Mother was.

Even after I had received a great number of proposals of marriage and the men had all told me that I was the most beautiful girl they had ever seen, I was still doubtful. Perhaps I was only convinced I was beautiful when the Press referred to me as a 'Social Beauty'.

Therefore I wanted to make sure that my child, if she was a daughter, was beautiful from the time she was born.

I not only prayed that she would be but bought a very attractive picture of a baby which I had by my bed. I looked at it every day and when my first visitors came after Raine was born, they all said: 'Oh, you have had her painted already.'

This confirmed my conviction that you can influence your child from the moment it 'quickens' inside you.

I was also determined that she should be very clever and I read a lot of history books when I was expecting her. But I refused to read the most popular book of the day called *No Orchids for Miss Blandish*, which I felt was somewhat improper and she must not have her mind soiled by it.

As was usual in those days I had my baby at home. When the pains began the nurse sent for the doctor and I had the top surgeon who had attended to Royalty.

He was charming but I was furious with him because he refused to give me any chloroform. I could not understand why I should suffer such agony and pain when I should have been given some sort of anaesthetic.

What actually happened was that the child had the cord round her neck. Eventually I wondered why a woman was screaming and making such a noise. I had no idea it was me.

Raine was born black as they expected, with the cord round her neck. When she began to breathe they found she had eczema on her body which all the

McCorquodales have especially when they grow older.

She was certainly very lovely and at two months old she was photographed by Dorothy Wilding, the forerunner of Cecil Beaton. It was voted the most beautiful photograph of a Mother and Child ever taken.

Dorothy Wilding, because she admired me so much, photographed me every year for nothing. An exhibition of her photographs was held in London in 1992, and I had nineteen photographs on show, including the one of me with Raine as a baby.

Raine was as beautiful as I expected her to be. I was quite certain that my prayers and care for her brain would be equally effective.

I was not mistaken. She had a brilliant brain from the moment she went to school and had five distinctions which today would be the same as five 'A' Levels.

She later became Chairman of the English Heritage Committee and also was a Member of the Westminster City Council, where everyone said she was outstanding.

She had also learnt to understand people, which was more important than anything else. My Mother had taught her that we must always help others if we possibly can.

Therefore when her second husband, the Earl Spencer fell seriously ill and had an operation for a brain haemorrhage, he was saved, he always told me, entirely by Raine's devotion.

Although he was unconscious, she spent hours with him every day and talked to him as though he could understand. She told him all that was happening, what she had been doing, and who was enquiring after him.

He said to me later, that although he could not understand all that she had said, the mere fact that she was there talking to him kept him alive and made him recover.

Lord Mountbatten told me that he had known this happen on other occasions with people who were completely unconscious, yet they knew that someone they loved was talking to them.

My son-in-law, Johnnie, always said that it was solely due to Raine that he was alive.

Later there was a Thanksgiving Service at the Church of All Saints, Northampton, for the Recovery of Edward John, 8th Earl Spencer.

Sir John Mills, film star and friend of the family, read the lesson, and Leader of the House of Commons, Mr. Norman St. John Stevas gave the address, and also referred to the unceasing work of Countess Spencer.

The Rt. Rev. Mervyn Stockwood, who was the Bishop of Southwark, took the service, which was attended by doctors and nurses who had cared for the Earl as well as local dignitaries.

Raine has now married again for the third time and is Comtesse Jean François de Chambrun.

She speaks fluent French as I had her taught Parisian French, something I had never learnt myself but had always regretted.

She has, however, always avoided publicity with the exception of when she made a fuss at London Airport which hit the headlines, because the cups and saucers were so dirty in the tea shop. Otherwise she has always told me not to talk to the Press about her.

When she brought Comte Jean François de Chambrun to meet me I was astonished to find a crowd of people waiting outside the door.

I asked them what they wanted and they said they were the Press.

I asked in horror, 'Who has asked you to come here?' To which they replied, 'Her Ladyship's lady's maid.'

I went indoors but said nothing and merely waited for the newly engaged couple to arrive.

The Comte was charming and had the beautiful manners which all Frenchmen have.

When I said how sorry I was that the Press were outside, to my amazement they were both delighted. They went outside, talked to the Press and finally when a second lot arrived they kissed in front of them. This was a complete change from what I had known before.

I admit I was very astonished at the excitement over her wedding from the time she was mobbed when she attended the Register Office in London where there was an enormous crowd of Press, to when she was married with bridesmaids and a special singer from Europe in the church near her son's home in Somerset.

The Press, of course, had the last word.

When I left the church there was a huge crowd of journalists who rushed towards me to ask me my impressions of the wedding.

I said:

'They are very much in love with each other and we must all pray that they will live happily ever afterwards.'

In printing it, however, the Press took off the last words, and quoted me as saying:

'They are very much in love and we must all pray for them!' Raine told me that the Comte was not amused.

At sixty-three, Raine's face is still lovely and, swimming in the Mediterranean with the Comte regularly, she has got very much thinner.

In fact a man described her to me the other day and said that she looked 'like a girl of sixteen'.

But, as her friends say, she still has 'all her wits about her'.

She has joined two committees in Nice and I am sure they will benefit from her brilliant brain, as London benefited when she was working here.

I had received a total of fifty-five proposals before I married the fifty-sixth in 1936 although actually my second husband had loved me for eight years before I finally said 'yes'.

Hugh McCorquodale was the first cousin of my first husband, Alexander, whom I divorced in 1933. It was very romantic that he had fallen in love with me when he saw me for the first time signing the Register in St Margaret's, Westminster at my first marriage.

He loved me for eight years and then having had a great number of other proposals I realised that he was so much part of my life that it was impossible to live without him.

He was a very quiet, charming man who had been terribly wounded at the battle of Passchendaele. I was told I would only have five years with him as he would not live any longer.

Actually I had twenty-seven years of blissful happiness.

He was as anxious to have children as I was. I have always been quite certain that my eldest son, Ian, was conceived in a blue train travelling from Paris to Cannes where we spent the second part of our honeymoon.

As I can never have my babies without undue excitement, Ian was born with an hour-glass contraction, which is very rare and which my gynaecologist had only seen once before in his whole career.

They were therefore delighted with me but I was so thrilled to have a son that they were afraid I was going to get up and dance.

Ian was a beautiful baby and I am quite certain because I was so excited and thrilled when he was on the way that his brain and his brilliant way of thinking up new ideas started when I prayed that he would be good-looking, clever and original in himself.

After my husband died, Ian left McCorquodales where he had learnt a great deal about printing and became my manager.

Since then he has got my books into almost every country in the world and is always thinking up astounding new ideas.

At the moment Ian is introducing me in a new way to China and has ideas for other distant nations where I have never been published before.

Ian has two daughters, Iona and Tara, and I very much hope that he will have a son as clever as himself who will carry on not only the family name but also the family pictures I have managed to collect over the years. It would be a tragedy for them to be lost or scattered as they were before I found them.

My second son, Glen, is very much like his Father.

He is quiet, gentle, very good-tempered, yet has positive ideas on what is right and what is wrong.

Like my husband he would never stoop to doing anything which was crooked, or in common parlance 'sharp'. He dislikes publicity, just as my husband did, and disappears at the sight of a camera.

He is, however, excellent where it concerns money as he worked for some years on the Stock Exchange. He is now in complete charge of my financial affairs and I know that he will carry out his work not only brilliantly but completely within the rules which so few people keep today.

He, too, was born in a difficult way like my other two children.

In fact we had moved to stay with Lady Delamere at Six Mile Bottom owing to the war driving us out of London.

With the usual extraordinary manner of those at the top, the gynaecologist who had brought Raine and Ian into the world, and also a great number of the Royal Family, was sent to look after old people in Sussex.

I wrote to him in despair saying:

'What shall I do? You know I must have someone as good as you, otherwise I might have lost my two other children.'

He wrote back saying there was a very famous gynaecologist in Cambridge but he would only take on difficult cases. He suggested I went to see him.

I did as he told me and promised the gynaecologist that I would provide him with a pink elephant with five legs if he would undertake to look after me when I had the baby.

He laughed and said he could not refuse an offer like that and he would come to Six Mile Bottom when the local doctor sent for him.

Glen was born on December 31st 1939. There was three feet of snow outside and I had two nurses and two doctors to attend to me.

I was very fortunate that the famous man had condescended to attend me as I had what was known as placenta privea which means that the afterbirth comes away first and they had great difficulty in bringing out the child.

However, when finally holding Glen in my arms my husband was allowed to see me and he was as thrilled as I was at having another son.

Glen has travelled all round the world with me and he looks after me beautifully.

He has a way of his own in getting what he wants by being charming rather than aggressive.

We are always very happy together and each year since I have been older we have motored in Europe enjoying the magnificent food of the French and stopping where there is art which Glen enjoys more than any other member of the family.

It is wonderful for me to have two men I admire and love, and who love me, to work with and know that whatever I do will not only help the family, but help the many people who write to me because my books have brought happiness and what we all seek, which is 'Love'.

My Mother, who was a wonderful person, always believed we should become head of something.

'It does not matter what you are top of,' she said, 'but you must succeed at something even if it is tiddly-winks.'

We were therefore brought up to feel we had to do something to please her.

She herself was absolutely marvellous in that when she became a Roman Catholic she was Chairman of the Catholic organization, 'The Sword and Spirit' for six counties.

When she died the Archbishop of Birmingham came to bury her and six other priests joined in. The Archbishop wore white robes because he knew I did not like black and started his address by saying:

'This is a very happy day.'

She was ninety-eight and a half when she died.

Locally, people mourned her for a very long time. People still come up to me and say how wonderful she was and how much she helped them. She helped them with herself rather than her money because she was never very well off.

I thought it very important that my children should aim for something as we had been told to do when I was a child.

I believe the most important thing of all is for people to learn to speak well. After all if you are fighting for something which is unjust, as I have done, you have to be able to express yourself eloquently, otherwise people do not understand what you are fighting for.

I remember my Father became a very good speaker after he was Knight of the Primrose League for six counties.

He was determined, if he survived the war, which he did not as he was killed in 1918, to enter Parliament.

My brother Ronald, at the age of three, would stand on a chair and pretend he was speaking to people in front of him.

When he entered the House of Commons he astounded them all by making the most brilliant speeches, although he was only twenty-seven at the time.

When Ronald was missing at Dunkirk, the Prime Minister, Winston Churchill, rang my Mother three times personally to ask if there was any news of him.

He said that if Ronald returned he was going to give him a Ministry.

Ronald's speeches were marvellous and the Earl of Selbourne and I put them together in a booklet called *The Common Problem* which was sold for Mrs. Churchill's Fund for Russia.

I was therefore determined my children should speak well, without being nervous.

It is nerves which upset everyone and that is why I have always remembered an incident in my life when I was nine.

It was the General Election of 1910.

In those days instead of building a platform for the speakers they used a huge farm cart. It was in the open field where they were holding a meeting.

I walked behind the cart, although I do not know why, and I saw a man sitting on it with shaking hands and chattering teeth.

I looked at him in surprise and said:

'Are you ill?'

He replied:

'No ... I am ... always like ... this ... before I make a ... speech.'

I learnt later his name was Stanley Baldwin and he became Prime Minister of this country.

Over the years I evolved a Christmas routine which because it is traditional becomes dearer to us year by year.

We have, of course, a Christmas tree, and I so much prefer a natural green one as they were when they were introduced to England at the suggestion of Queen Adelaide, wife of William IV.

Our presents are all arranged on the same chairs, year after year, in the drawing room. My earliest recollection of Christmas is being given, at the age of two, an enormous doll's house by my Grandmother, the one who was related to Robert the Bruce.

I can vividly recall going into her bedroom because she was ill and there was the doll's house at the foot of her bed. It seemed to me to be enormous. It opened and had two storeys with a kitchen, drawing room, and bedrooms all containing tiny dolls. I think that that, at the age of two, made me love big houses for the rest of my life.

I also remember the stockings I used to find at the end of my bed when I awoke on Christmas morning.

My Father and Mother had crept in very quietly

and filled one of my Father's shooting stockings which were of course large and long.

The difficulty for every child is not to wake up too early and enjoy the presents in the dark. But one goes to bed believing that Father Christmas will really come.

Most important of all at Christmas dinner now we have speeches from the youngest to the oldest male.

They were usually nine when they were old enough to come down to dinner and for the first year my sons were allowed to write their speech. After that it had to be extemporary.

They thought it great fun and, if you can get over your family giggling and laughing at you, after that the Albert Hall presents no difficulties.

My eldest son is a brilliant speaker and my second son is very witty.

My Grandson William is asked to speak all over the country when a Member of Parliament falls ill.

My Grandson Rupert won the Debating Cup at the Bar.

All this, I am convinced, is due to the fact they learnt to speak when they were young, and find it no trouble now they are older.

What I learnt myself was to speak fluently without being nervous and of course I had to do it the hard way.

I helped my brother win the Labour-held seat of King's Norton, in Birmingham, and my job, which I always think is a depressing one, was to hold the attention of the audience until the prospective candidate arrived from the previous meeting.

One watches the door anxiously hoping he will

soon appear and wondering if you will run out of ideas before he arrives.

Then of course when he does come you move on to the next place and hold another audience until he reappears.

I did this for Ronald and I also did it during the war for the Member of Parliament for Bedfordshire who was Alan Lennox-Boyd, later Lord Boyd.

After my brother was killed at Dunkirk I was offered three Conservative seats, all safe ones.

But I had three young children – the youngest still a baby – and a husband.

I knew that it was wrong to leave them so much even though I would have loved to be a Member of Parliament.

I therefore refused the offer and, in 1955, became a Member of the Hertfordshire County Council when we moved here after Raine was married.

I won the seat at Hatfield, which was Labour held, for the Conservatives and during the nine years I was their County Councillor I had the Law of England changed three times.

This was due, I am certain, to the fact that I am a good speaker because I have had so much experience.

What I undertook was certainly tough. It required a great deal of speaking and arguing and trying to convince people I was right.

The first was to do with the old people who were being very badly treated, because there was not enough money being spent on them to make them comfortable.

I visited a great many Homes in Hertfordshire and my daughter went round 250 Homes all over the country making reports on them. They were all the same, needing more money than they were already receiving.

It was not a popular request, I can assure you, but finally I had a letter from the Minister, Duncan Sandys saying:

'Here is the Gospel according to St. Barbara,' and he gave them more money.

The man who had been previously responsible for the Homes in Hertfordshire came up to me, I thought very courageously, and said:

'I hated you because I thought you were undoing the good I had done in the Homes. But now I realise we need more money and I am very, very grateful.'

I thought it extremely brave of him to say so and I was very touched.

The second one was far more difficult.

I learnt that since the time of Henry VIII when gypsies first came to this country the children had never been able to go to school, because the police moved their caravans every twenty-four hours.

I found the first gypsies I had really talked to sitting on a common near Hatfield.

They said they had been born there and had always returned wherever else they had been.

They were sitting on the grass listening to the schools' broadcast.

They showed me a summons they had just been given for having a dustbin, two milk churns and a pram containing a live baby.

I went home and rang up the Chief Constable of Police, who had already helped me in a number of other problems. I said to him now:

'These people appear to be law-abiding. They don't want to get into trouble. Where can they go?'

'Nowhere,' he answered.

'Nowhere?' I echoed. 'But that is absurd. They have been told they have to move every twenty-four hours, and if they can go nowhere it means a perpetual life of wandering. Besides, they are flesh and blood, they can't just disintegrate.'

'I am sorry,' he said, 'but that is the law as it stands. The Police are as sympathetic as they can be, but you can understand we are being pressed all the time by local people who don't like gypsies to move them on.

'Almost as soon as a caravan stops anywhere someone will be on the telephone to the police station demanding that they move the next day.'

'It is absolutely ridiculous,' I retorted. 'If that is the law then it is time it was changed and somehow I will change it.'

The following month I attended the Divisional Sessions in St. Albans. The policeman read out the charges and the magistrates allowed me to speak.

I said that as a County Councillor I thought the gypsies ought to be rewarded not fined for having a dustbin.

'We keep begging people to put their litter into a dustbin and yet when they have one we try to charge them for it. I can't imagine anything so ridiculous.'

I also asked the magistrates if they knew where the gypsies could go as they didn't want to break the law.

The magistrates looked embarrassed and mumbled that they were there only to 'administer justice'.

But that did not stop them fining Luke Davis £3 for camping and driving a lorry on the Common, although they dismissed the charge of litter.

At the next meeting of the County Council I asked if a reserve or camp could be provided for the gypsies of Hertfordshire.

I told the Councillors there were a large number of true gypsies in the county and that it was essential the children who were Hertfordshire born should be given an education.

It was a three-year battle and a very fierce one as people have an unreasonable dislike of gypsies.

Unfortunately there are many people nowadays who pretend to be gypsies but who are often drug-takers and make trouble wherever they go.

Finally after three years I had a letter from Sir Keith Joseph, to say I had won!

I was absolutely thrilled.

Now we have fifteen camps for gypsies in Hertfordshire alone and I have my own camp where there are the original Romany gypsies I found with the dustbin, and they have been very happy there ever since.

What has interested me perhaps more than anything else is that when I contacted the schools to see how they had got on more or less every schoolmaster said the same.

'They come to school clean and tidy and look upon education as a privilege.'

What really pleased me was that the parents have now learnt to read and write because the children have been to school.

Instead of sending someone down to read a letter

when I write to my gypsies, I can now not only telephone but they can read everything I send them.

This is a tremendous step forward and I believe and hope it is happening in every county as well as it is in Hertfordshire.

The third time I altered the law was again a very hard battle.

I discovered that for seven years Prayers had been taken out of State schools.

No one had protested and there had not been one murmur from the Church.

I started to write about it in various articles and finally after a year or so had passed, the *Daily Star* not only published my article but sent it by hand to every Member of Parliament.

One is not allowed to hand letters in to be passed round to each Member. They have to be addressed to Mr Brown, Mr Smith and Mr Jones.

I then received over three hundred letters in reply headed by young Winston Churchill in which they said they had no idea that the Prayers had been taken out of the schools.

They were astonished that no one had told them and therefore voted both in the House of Lords and in the House of Commons that there should be PrayersandReligiousEducationinalltheStateschools.

What of course always happens when one is pleased and delighted over something which has been a long battle is that the enemy creeps in once again.

This time it was the Humanists and they have, at the moment – as far as I know although there may be more – made five hundred videos in which they say they have proved there is no God and you do not need to have prayers said over you when you die. They have sent them as a present to the schools who have accepted them. So far there has been no action taken against it except by me.

All this has been happening since I came to Camfield Place.

When Raine got married in 1948 after being a great success as the most beautiful and best-dressed debutante of the year – I remember at that time we were still on coupons which proved extremely difficult – my husband said to me:

'Thank goodness, we can now go to the country.'

We found a house which was very attractive, standing in four hundred acres. I could not believe when I saw it that it was not only beautiful inside but had ten bathrooms. Up to the time of the war there were few bathrooms in gentlemen's houses.

In fact when I was looking for a house in London for Raine to 'come out', in which I wanted to be able to give a ball for her, I went all down Park Lane.

The only bathroom they had in the houses was usually pushed away in the servants' quarters and was very small and extremely dingy.

I was thrilled to come to Camfield Place to find it had a very exciting history of its own.

The Romans used the gravel from the ground and a Roman road crosses the lakes.

In 1275 a Knight called Camfield settled down in what is now 'the Green Belt'.

In Queen Elizabeth's reign the owner built a delightful Tudor house with a large dovecote.

This existed until 1867 when Beatrix Potter's

Grandfather came down from the North. Rich and without much taste – he pulled down most of the Tudor house.

He then built a large mansion leaving only Beatrix Potter's bedroom and her sitting room as part of the original house.

Another owner just before I came to Camfield was Lord Queenborough.

He fortunately had two millionaire American wives. They created Georgian cornices and parquet flooring in every room. They also added the most beautiful and exquisite mantelpieces. The one in the drawing room was designed by the Adam Brothers in the 1700s.

What is more, being American wives they had ten bathrooms added to the house between them.

This, of course, was because before World War I ladies always bathed in their bedrooms.

I remember as a child the footman carrying upstairs brass cans which had to be polished every day, and filled with hot and cold water.

They put them outside the bedroom and the house-maids brought them in and poured them into the bath, which had been arranged before the fire.

It was a delightful and very luxurious way of having a bath! But after the War, when people were poor, and staff were scarce, it was extremely imprac-tical.

I was thrilled with my ten bathrooms, and also to find that Beatrix Potter had written a fascinating letter about Camfield Place to her Grandmother:

To me all is bound up together in fact and fancy,

my dear grandmother, the place I love best in the world and the sweet balmy air where I have been so happy as a child. I shall never want a record to remind me of this perfect whole, where all things are a part, the notes of the stable clock and the all pervading smell of new-mown hay, the distant sounds of the farmyard.

Certainly I and my family have been very happy all the years we have been at Camfield Place.

I had the house blessed when I came in by a clergyman who had been in Jamaica where they always bless their houses. So we have no ghosts which frightened Beatrix Potter, except a dog who was put to sleep after the blessing, and who stays with us because he loves us.

I see him from time to time.

When Beatrix was sitting in the drawing room, working on the tiny code she used for writing her books, which took six years to break, the lights, which were twelve candles, went out one by one as if snuffed by an invisible hand!

Her Grandmother quite unperturbed rang the bell for a footman to light them again.

When I came here Lord Queenborough had built the most beautiful library. It is blue picked out in white and the books are behind glass.

It is very elegant, but alas! I now have over six thousand books and every bedroom and every bathroom has shelves bulging with them. As I am now published in virtually every country in the world, we have foreign books stored away in the attics, and in every other part of the house.

But when I walk in Mr. McGregor's Garden and look at the door in the wall which 'the fat little rabbit could not squeeze underneath' and down the Nut Walk, which when I came was full of pretty red squirrels, I think that just as it was the most perfect place on earth to Beatrix, so it is to me.

It certainly enables me to write of love and as I finished my six-hundredth book, I felt I was sending out from Camfield some of the beauty and love which is inherent here for ever.

My beloved husband, Hugh, died suddenly at Camfield on 29 December 1963, one day after we had celebrated twenty-seven years of great happiness.

Once I said to him:

'If a fairy could wave a magic wand and give you anything you wanted, what would you wish to have?'

Hugh thought for a moment and replied:

'I have everything I have ever wanted.'

He loved me deeply but he believed that death was the end of everything: there was no after-life, no meeting in another world with those we loved.

After his death I had a message which told me he had been mistaken. I have written down exactly what happened so that it will help other people.

On July 31st 1917, at the Third Battle of Ypres, 2nd Lieut. Hugh McCorquodale received the Military Cross – 'for his gallantry and devotion to duty during the action. It was largely due to his fine personal example and skilful handling of his Company that the enemy counter-attack was delayed.'

My husband was just nineteen years old when he was posted to the 6th Battalion in Flanders. Two

months later came the terrible slaughter at Passchendaele.

In this battle the expectation of a subaltern's life
was twenty minutes.

On July 31st there were 279 casualties in the battalion, and Hugh was severely – almost mortally –
wounded. In attacking the enemy trenches he was
hit with a sniper's dum-dum bullet which passed
right through his right shoulder and out of his back
exploding as it went.

This among other injuries, collapsed his lung and
smashed three ribs. He turned head over heels and
lay out in No Man's Land for forty-eight hours.

'You were very near to death,' I said to him when
we were married. 'Did you see angels, hear voices,
or even feel you were being helped or sustained?'

'No,' he replied. 'I just felt very tired and far away
from all the noise of the battle.'

During the second night Hugh was carried in on a
man's back and received a number of shrapnel
wounds in the process.

At the Field Dressing Station they treated only
the shrapnel wounds, not realising he was injured
elsewhere. He was carried down to the base, but
the shelling was so bad that the stretcher-bearers
dropped him continually.

When he eventually arrived at No. 9 Red Cross
Hospital at Calais he was so covered in mud they
did not realise he was an officer and he was, at first,
put in the Tommies' ward.

When the doctors examined Hugh they said there
was nothing they could do and there was not a
chance of his survival. He was therefore, as was the

practice in those days, put outside in a tent in the grounds of the hospital by himself to die.

On August 25th, his uncle, General Lord Horne (of Stirkoke) who was commanding the First Army, was informed.

He sent for Hugh's parents to come over from England to say 'Goodbye' to their son. Mr. and Mrs. Harold McCorquodale crossed the Channel and saw Hugh for what they thought was the last time.

Hugh had fortunately been taken to a 'rich' hospital which was run by the Canadians, and they gave him port and champagne when they dressed his wounds and the rest of the time he was under heroin.

He lay for four weeks without food, in a state of semi-consciousness, and we now know that leaving him alone and letting him get over the shock was what saved his life.

After attending five hospitals and having innumerable operations, Hugh survived.

He was a 'show piece' for the doctors, as they considered it a tremendous achievement that they had kept him alive, and he remembered being constantly 'shown off' to visiting specialists.

When he was discharged the doctors said to him:

'It is a miracle you are alive. Nothing more can be done by surgery, so never let anyone fiddle about with you. You must trust to nature and live with your disability.'

It was advice he was to stick to all his life and gave him what amounted to almost a fear of doctors.

Hugh was listed as 40 per cent disabled and received a pension which, at the time of his death, was £185. 16s. 0d a year!

His convalescence was very slow and when I met him first in 1927 I was told by various members of his family, including his mother, that he was not expected to live long and if he ever got influenza he would die.

We often talked about 'the after-life' especially when my brothers Ronald and Tony were both killed at Dunkirk.

'Do you really believe,' I would say to my husband, 'that all Ronald's struggle to help other people is wasted? The times he went hungry so that he could buy books on politics? The years he spent in the Research Department of the Conservative Central Office? The difficulties of money, of working until he made himself ill because he could not afford a secretary? Has all that hope, ambition, energy and faith died with him?'

'I am afraid so,' my husband would answer.

As I have said he was a very quiet, gentle man, who never forced his opinions on anyone, but if I asked him what he thought, he always told me the truth.

On December 29th 1963, after two days of slight bronchitis Hugh got out of bed and collapsed. The scar tissues from the terrible wounds he had received in 1917 had touched his heart.

The day before, though, the doctor said there was no need for anxiety, but I was instinctively alarmed and I rang Mrs Gibson, a healer.

I told her about Hugh and she promised to ring me back.

When she did so she said:

'I must be honest, dear, and tell you there is nothing

I can do: his time has come. I have covered him in blue and he will pass peacefully.'

I did not believe her and slammed down the telephone.

I had always known Hugh's life hung on a thread and I was deeply grateful for having had him with me for so long.

He did not suffer and for him it was the peaceful, quick death he would have wanted. But that did not assuage the ghastly shock and the terrible sense of loss. I had never seen anyone dead before – all my family had died in France.

As I stood beside him as he lay in a blue bed wearing blue pyjamas, I could not believe, when he had loved me so much, that he had left me alone.

A week after the funeral my maid, who had been with me for over twenty-five years, said:

'Have you noticed the wonderful scent of carnations outside Mr McCorquodale's dressing room?'

'No,' I replied. 'Are you sure? There have not been any carnations in the house since the funeral and those in the wreaths had no fragrance, not in December.'

'I was so surprised at the strength of the perfume,' my maid went on, 'that I called the daily woman and drew her attention to it. She smelt it too but said it must be something someone had put in their bath.'

I did not think any more about this conversation, but the next morning I got up at seven o'clock as usual to give my son Glen his breakfast before he left for London.

There is an entresol with only a skylight outside my bedroom on to which opened the doors from my husband's dressing room, his bathroom and the room in which he died.

As I crossed the entresol I was suddenly aware of the marvellous, almost overpowering scent of carnations. It was unlike any carnations I had ever smelt in England – it was the true exotic fragrance of Malmaisons which I had not known for years.

I stood for a moment feeling astounded, then had to hurry downstairs in case Glen missed his train. When he had gone, I went upstairs and the scent was still there but fainter.

I thought I must have imagined it but the following morning it was there again. It was, I discovered, in patches, the strongest scent being next to my husband's dressing room. Some mornings it was not there at all, or I could not smell it until I returned upstairs after breakfast.

The fragrance came and went for three weeks.

I asked a friend of mine who had been a medium if she noticed anything, not saying what I was thinking. She identified the unmistakable scent of Malmaison carnations and found it all round my bedroom door.

I then knew exactly why it was there.

My husband and I had always bought red carnations when we went abroad. Every year we went to Paris for a Second Honeymoon. The first thing we would do on arrival was to drive to the Madeleine. Outside there are always rows of colourful flower stalls.

Hugh would buy me a huge bunch of red carnations before we went into the Church of the Sacré Coeur which is the only church I have ever known which has a chapel to Saint Joseph who is the Patron

Saint of Marriage, in which we said a prayer for our marriage. This was something we had done on our first honeymoon and repeated every year except during the war.

The carnations would be arranged in my bedroom. Each evening when we went out to dinner Hugh would wear one in his buttonhole. If anything was a symbol of our happiness and our closeness to each other, it was red carnations.

Now I understood why the scent of them was near my door. It could only mean one thing, that Hugh was trying to tell me he had been wrong.

He had found a way to convey to me the truth – there is an after-life, there *is* survival after death.

Few people realize that when a man has been wounded and his blood circulation has been shortened, he is far more passionate than is normal.

The Amazons never had any use for men, but they always broke the legs of their prisoners because it made them better lovers.

Nelson was not an impressive looking man, but he had lost his arm, and it made him a fantastic lover.

There was a man in the twenties who was a gentleman and had been in The Guards, but he was very ordinary and nobody paid much attention to him.

I remember that he was running to catch a train when it was moving and a porter tried to stop him.

In the struggle he fell from the platform and his legs were both damaged.

After this he became one of the most sought-after men in London, and one beauty after another fell into his arms. No party was complete without him.

Duncan Sandys had a fantastic reputation after his foot was run over by an English – not German – tank!

# Chapter Two

I n 1978 my daughter had married for the second time, to Earl Spencer. My eldest son was also married and had two children. Therefore my youngest son Glen and I decided to travel.

We had already discovered a great deal of the world – including seeing the world at 14,000 feet from a train over the Andes when we visited Peru and Bolivia.

Another time we found something new and different when we went to Haiti, which is famous for its voodoo. When we arrived we found we were staying at a very comfortable hotel. We were able to eat dinner outside in the moonlight which was very romantic.

We went to a building where quite a number of people had congregated with the kind of expressions on their faces which always occurs when something supernatural is happening and they are not certain whether they approve of it or not.

The performance of those who were dancing to the voodoo music made everything shake as they shouted again and again. They then drank from a black bottle and blew out white clouds from their mouths. This we were told was *clarin*, a native white rum which would burn itself not only into a man's mouth, but into his mind.

We watched all this with great interest and it was obvious that the audience was captivated. When they asked me if I would like to go to a special performance later on in the evening I refused.

Instead the next day we travelled through the woods and I was promised by our guide that we would see wilder and more exotic voodoos.

We were fortunate enough to meet Katherine Dunham who knows more about voodoo than anyone else in the country. A famous black ballerina now retired, she had her own Voodoo Temple in the garden of her beautiful home.

We also attended the temple belonging to Jean Beauvoir, a Doctor of Science. We saw a performance given by his voodoo adepts, although we were not allowed to stay for a private ceremony given afterwards, which was only for the initiated. The dancing was sensational, the drums mesmeric.

Voodoo, which is now allowed by law in Haiti, concerns, we were told, over sixty per cent of the population. Catholicism and Voodoo meet on what is nearly common ground.

We enjoyed our visit to Haiti enormously although I felt that underneath there was a creepy atmosphere in which I would not like to live for very long.

We left taking with us many souvenirs including a metrodite thunderstone, which is kept in every temple and in the possession of every priest or *papaloi* and which Katherine Dunham had given me.

However, as it had a strange mark on it which I thought was a fault, I became suspicious that it might not be as lucky as she thought it was. I therefore threw it away under water which I have always believed prevents anything magical from affecting us one way or another.

I have always enjoyed travelling, and some very strange things happened to my brother Ronald and I whenever we went abroad.

One particular incident on a holiday in Austria will always remain in my mind as being rather frightening.

Seeboden is a small village on the banks of a warm lake in Carinthia. Ronald and I had planned to go to Millstatt, a larger place, but when we arrived we thought it too big and crowded.

We hired a taxi and eventually found Seeboden, our task complicated by the fact that we spoke no German and hardly anyone knew a word of English.

Attached to a villa we saw a little wooden chalet.

We were determined it should be ours. Rooms in Austria are let by the bed – the idea, therefore, being to pack as many beds as possible in a room.

Being a poor people they think nothing of sharing.

In the villa, for instance, a judge, his wife and their three children, all over fifteen, shared a room together.

When Ronald and I asked for a whole room each they simply could not understand our wild extravagance.

'You want one room – two beds, yes?' they would insist.

Finally, by bribery and corruption we obtained the chalet, which had a room downstairs with a balcony overlooking the lake, a room upstairs, and – joy of joys! – a private lavatory.

The top room had been taken by a so-called 'engaged couple' who moved with the utmost good humour into the boathouse, where on wet nights they slept with an umbrella over their heads since the roof leaked.

The Austrians are a delightful people, so kind and so good-natured, as almost to make one want to shake them and tell them to stick up for their rights.

We were at a café on the lakeside while a band played and where the chief dishes were young deer shot in the surrounding forests and *wilden beeren* (wild berries).

We had those too, for breakfast every morning, with hot rolls and a huge jug of steaming coffee served with great spoonfuls of whipped cream.

The mornings we spent bathing and sunbathing, watching with amusement the guests at the villa come down to the lake with cakes of soap with which to wash themselves.

In the afternoons we used to walk up the steep sides of the mountains, finding attractive little villages where the coffee was beyond praise and where the church was always beautiful.

The wood carving over the altars and on the pulpits was often coloured but always in perfect taste. We never saw anything tawdry or even ugly in those ancient buildings.

We found too, it was easy to pray in them, the

faithful who had worshipped there for generations had left a living impression of the God they loved.

Then as the sun was sinking and we felt the cold, chill air from the distant snows, we hurried home passing Calvaries and lowing cattle, to the welcoming lights and music of the lakeside cafés.

One day as we walked round the lake we were caught in a thunderstorm: the beating rain, blinding flashes of lightning and the tempestuous waves were really quite terrifying.

Then, as suddenly as it had arrived, the storm subsided and the sun shone on the rain-washed country with a dazzling brilliance.

As we hurried home to change our soaked clothes we saw on the other side of the lake the most magnificent castle.

It was white with a black roof surmounted by a flag floating in the breeze.

Against the background of green hills, it rose until in the distance one could see the white peaks shimmering against the blue sky. It was lovely beyond words.

It had, too, an enchantment, as if the fairy palaces one had dreamt of in the nursery had come to life.

'I must go there,' I told Ronald. 'I want to see the inside of an Austrian castle for my new book.'

We sat on a seat to look at it.

'Oh, dear, I am afraid the flag is flying,' I remarked. 'The Herr Baron himself must be in residence.'

'We can but try to get in,' Ronald said. 'We will go there tomorrow.'

The next afternoon we set off. We could not find the castle.

The following day we tried again and we eventually discovered it – in ruins!

There were Gothic archways, the remains of a tower, the foundations of a great courtyard, the first steps of a twisting staircase.

But there was no wall more than eight feet tall, each one being of grey, crumbling stone covered with moss and ivy.

How had we seen for over an hour the previous afternoon the castle as it had once been in all its splendour?

Later I thought perhaps it was a message which I had not understood at the time.

It has made it easier in many ways to recognise the signs I have had from Ronald that he is still thinking of me, helping me and I believe waiting until we meet again.

While I am writing about my visits I must tell you about one of the most interesting which was to Russia in 1978.

It was entirely through Lord Mountbatten that I visited Russia.

In fact, it had never occurred to me to do so until he asked me to accompany him to a cocktail party to which he had been invited at the Soviet Embassy.

Because I was curious to see the Embassy and had in fact met few Russians, I was only too delighted to go with him.

He suggested that I should dress very quietly. But it seemed to me a mistake to play down to a communistic idea of how women should look.

I therefore wore something in bright pink which I had adopted as a special colour for me ever since in

1927 I visited Egypt for the first time and found Howard Carter sitting on the tomb of Tutankhamen which he had recently discovered with Lord Carnarvon.

Because he thought I was interesting and I think very pretty, he personally took me round the tombs of the Kings. I was thrilled with the wonderful colours of the reliefs on the walls which were mostly very bright pink and scarab blue. They became the two colours which I felt inspired me.

I wear them and they are the main colours in my home.

While we were at the Embassy, where they were delighted to see Lord Mountbatten, the Ambassador asked me if I had ever been to Russia.

I replied I had not but I hoped I would go there one day and perhaps write a novel about it.

A few days later the Embassy telephoned Lord Mountbatten's Secretary and asked if I was serious in wishing to go to Russia in which case they would arrange a special visit for me.

It was of course a fascinating idea. As I have already said I and my youngest son Glen were exploring the world and in 1978 thought we should also explore Russia.

I felt I was on a good wicket in that they had asked Lord Mountbatten if I would go. I told his Secretary to say I would go but on certain conditions.

Firstly, that I could travel First Class on Aeroflot, which they did not have. However, they gave me the first two rows of seats and I had caviare and champagne all the way to Leningrad.

I also said I was too old to go through customs

which I was told were long and dreary in Russia.

When we arrived at Leningrad there was a car waiting for me outside the airport. There was a man to look at my passport, another to see what money I had and a third to pass my luggage. I then drove off while the rest of the passengers were still moving into the Customs House.

'If this is Communism,' I said to Glen, 'it is certainly very comfortable.'

We stayed at a delightful hotel where they had been told I complained that they took a long time with the food.

The food was more or less always the same. There was caviare to start with, chicken Kiev to follow and ice-cream.

As I had said they were slow, they then brought me all three courses together so that by the time we had finished the chicken the ice-cream had melted away.

However, under the circumstances I dared not complain.

We were taken round Leningrad by the most charming and the most important of their guides who spoke perfect English and I think we missed nothing.

The Winter Palace was entrancing and so were the other palaces. What was amazing and what impressed me considerably was how they had restored the damage done by the Germans and made the palaces almost exactly as they had been originally.

I found it hard to believe that they could have found the craftsmen to replace the paintings and carvings which had been damaged by the war and which we were shown in photographs.

There were parties given for me in the evening to meet some extremely interesting Russians. I was allowed to drive in the car, with which I was provided, anywhere I wished to go with no restrictions.

Everyone was extremely pleasant to us. I asked my guides if there were any churches open in Leningrad and they said that there were seventeen.

They took me to one where I saw a lot of elderly women sitting outside and I did not understand why until I went inside.

A funeral, a wedding and a christening were all taking place at the same time. As it was rather a small church there was not enough room for them. It also made me think that perhaps the other churches were closed and not in use. That was the only one I was able to see.

We went by train from Leningrad to Moscow. We stayed in a hotel which looked on to Red Square.

I had learnt while I was in Russia that they thought Lord Mountbatten was Royal and always referred to him as a Prince. His name certainly brought magic where my son and I were concerned and everything was done to make us as comfortable as possible.

We visited the Kremlin and saw everything we wished to see without any difficulty.

When we left Russia and flew back to England it was hard to believe all the stories we had heard of the restrictions, discomforts and misery of Communism. At the same time there was no doubt that it was there beneath the surface.

We arrived home to find people looked on us as

being rather brave to have visited the Soviet Union and expected us to tell them of the misery which the Russians themselves were suffering. They were quite disappointed when we told them the truth.

Perhaps it would have been helpful if more English people had visited Russia when things were as peaceful as they were then.

There have been many unpleasant stories of what has occurred in Russia since, but I can only speak of it as I saw it. I had no idea at that time that I would be popular in Russia as a writer.

It is only now, this year, that I have signed a contract for three million books a year as the Russians are longing for love and romance.

It is very exciting as up to now France has been the best seller of my books. In fact, the French bought 1,200,000 last year. It only shows that gradually the need for real romance and not just sex is beginning to appear in unusual places.

Glen and I really love the Far East and when I visited Bangkok for the fourth time in 1982 I found it even more fascinating than I had before.

It has always been known as the 'Land of Smiles', and the Thai people welcome one, not only with smiles, but with the charming good manners which today one only finds in the East.

My son and I first went to The Oriental Hotel in Bangkok which is one of the best hotels in the world. Built around 1887 by two sea captains, it is now of course very much larger, but still has the marvellous River Menam Chow Phya flowing past it.

What they have been so clever about in the last few years is that they asked Louis Outhier, who I think is one of the best chefs in France and who has just received yet another accolade, to advise them about their food. He gave them his own chef, his manager and all his priceless recipes.

This means one can sit in the Normandy Restaurant, which is on top of the old part of the hotel, looking at the river with its great barges going up and down, with the lights at night making it look like a fairyland, and eat the best French cuisine.

Thailand owes so much to King Chulalongkorn who ascended the throne when he was fifteen in 1868, and by 1910 when he died had brought Siam, as it was then, completely into the modern world.

His reign was a revolution from the throne because then Siam had no schools, roads, railways, hospitals or well equipped military forces. The King introduced all these, sent his son and other young men abroad for foreign education, and himself made two European tours.

In Bangkok, however, the palace with its brilliantly gilded domes and towers, and Temple of the Emerald Buddha, which is really one piece of jade, still has a fairytale quality which one cannot find anywhere else.

Of course Thailand is famous for its Thai silk and when we visited Chiang Mai in the North, we went to the Thai Silk Factory with its wonderful colours which are so unique.

Chiang Mai is full of the most fascinating temples, and Thailand is the only Buddhist country I have visited where instead of just burning joss-sticks in front of the image of the Lord Buddha, the devout place tiny pieces of gold leaf on his body, and on the

immense Buddha's foot which often stands in front
of the statue. The result is very attractive – shimmering gold in the sunlight, and there is an atmosphere of faith in the temples, which is very moving.

Chiang Mai was a walled city which repelled its
enemies for many centuries, the chief among these
being the Burmese, and it was not until 1796 that
it joined with Siam and became part of this lovely
country.

From the North we travelled to the South to the
Gulf of Pattaya, where what was originally a fishing
village has now been transformed into a very
fashionable holiday resort.

It is difficult to describe how beautiful it is with
the graceful, curving stretch of brilliant white sand,
a tropical island surrounded by the darker blue of
the coral reef, with boats of every sort moving across
the deep blue sea.

Pattaya really came into existence because it was
where the Americans in Vietnam spent their leave.

The delicious fresh fish which is to be eaten everywhere in Thailand comes from here, and is full of
vitamins and goodness. I am quite certain the health,
and therefore the beaming happiness of the Thai
people, owes a great deal to their diet.

I, however, found one of my favourite health foods
when I visited H.R.H. Prince Wong Lumpaopong,
who was one of the great Ambassadors to Thailand,
but is now retired and has a beautiful garden where
he keeps his bees. His honey is very special, his bees
unusual, and they are literally spoken of as one of
the sights of Thailand.

The Prince and his delightful wife gave us a real

Thailand tea with delicious types of rice served with leaves fastened around them, and a pumpkin cake which was quite unlike anything I had ever eaten before.

As most of Thailand's people are vegetarians because they are Buddhists, they have an amazing choice of health-giving food from their vegetables which not only look beautiful, but are delightful to eat, and their fruit is of course fantastic.

If anything would persuade me to become a vegetarian, it would not only be because of the beauty of the Thai people, but because of their good humour, their charm, and of course their smiles!

Because I have grown more famous as the years passed by, it is amusing now to realise that I have my own special suite called after me in a Bangkok hotel.

It was in February 1986 that Glen and I were off on one of our trips again. We went back to Bangkok especially to see the suite at The Oriental Hotel which had been named after me.

I was told that the Japanese always wanted to stay in my suite when they were on their honeymoon, because it brought them good luck. It is a charming suite, but as I said when I went into it, there is not enough pink. Several other people have said the same.

I adored being in Bangkok and I loved the people who are all very friendly and anxious to please their visitors.

We had luncheon at the British Embassy which Lord Mountbatten told me years ago was one of the most attractive Embassies he had ever seen. We had various trips up and down the river to see places we had not visited previously. There is a fascination about Bangkok which draws me back over and over again.

In February 1980 Glen and I went off to Mexico. We stayed in Acapulco and found it delightful.

The temples were entrancing and I was compelled to write several books about Mexico.

One of them being *A Miracle in Mexico* in which I described the different religions of the people, of which there are a great number and each one with its own God.

The God Quetzalcoatl is the God of Life, the God of Rain, and the God of the Morning Star. Some Mexicans still, to this day, use the following form of Marriage Service, when the Indian priest will say:

Barefoot on the living earth with face to the living sun, a man and a woman in the presence of the Morning Star meet to be perfect in one another.

Lift your face and say: This man is my rain from Heaven.

Kneel, Señor, touch the earth and say: This woman is the earth to me.

Señorita, kiss the feet of this man and say: This man I will give strength to him and we shall be one throughout the long twilight and the Morning Star.

Señor, kiss the brow and touch the head of this woman and say: I will be her peace and her rescue and we shall be one in the long twilight and the Morning Star.

Then the priest puts the man's hand over the woman's eyes and her hand over his and says:

This man has met this woman with his body and the Star of his shape, and this woman has met this man with her body and the Star of her yearning and they are one, and Quetzalcoatl has blessed them and made them one with the Morning Star.

As the priest raises his arms the couple are married.

What we found particularly attractive in Acapulco was that we had our own swimming pool attached to our rooms at the hotel.

It was delightful to be able to swim in the cool water but I like a real bath and they economised by giving one only a spray instead of a bath you could lie down in.

At the same time there was such beauty all round one that you felt it was wrong to grumble.

India is a country which I have always loved. I had already visited Udaipur and Jaipur in 1974, and I could not resist going back there again, accompanied by Glen, this time to Hyderabad.

Hyderabad is a beautiful city with its strange rock formations, its fascinating palaces, perfumes, pearls and beautiful women.

While on a visit to the Char Minar we saw a wedding procession going past Lad Bazar where the exotic masalas, bangles and silvery-tinselly things are sold. We alighted and were soon in the midst of the procession. As I was preparing a book for Kodak with unusual photo combinations and colours, here were just the required costumes, people and setting!

I attended a reception which had been arranged for me by the Muslim Educational Society (Ladies Wing) at the Jubilee Hall.

Here I was received by girls who were beautifully dressed in Khara *dupattas*, old brocades and tissues glittering with old Karchobi work with sequins *salma*, *gokhru*, *chutki* on the borders and old family jewels.

I was led to the pavilion where the Nizams sat when they held their *durbars* and was garlanded and made to taste a bit of *misri* (sugar) and offered a trayful of *ashraffis* (made of marzipan to look like gold coins).

I never go to India without thinking of the very first day I arrived in 1959 and had luncheon with Pandit Nehru and his then unknown daughter Indira.

Later when Edwina Mountbatten died I had a letter from Pandit Nehru which I thought was very moving in which he said:

It is difficult to realise that Edwina has gone. She was so full of life and vitality and one could not associate death with her. She was here for about ten days before she went further east, and she was to return to Delhi on her way back this month.

I have to remind myself often that she is not coming back. And yet, the manner of her death was typical of her. She died as she had lived, full of life and energy and devoted to the work she had undertaken.

After my travels it was always wonderful to be back at Camfield Place and to be doing all the familiar things which one always does at home. In fact I wrote a poem which expressed in verse what it meant to me.

I've seen the pyramids in Egypt
Aztec ruins in Mexico,
The almond blossom in Japan
Round the temples of Kyoto.

The Chinese treasures in Taiwan
And the glory of Ankor Wat,
The Blue Mosque in Persia,
The floating market in Bangkok.

India's beauty is endless,
Pink Palaces in Jaipur,
The loveliness of the Taj Mahal
Carved gateways in Mysore.

I've visited many countries,
Bali is emerald green
But still to me Great Britain,
Is the loveliest place I've seen.

The white cliffs of Dover.
Piccadilly in the rain,
The stately homes, like Woburn,
The field of golden grain.

Flower-filled suburban gardens,
Stonehenge of mystic stone,
The silver lakes of Windermere!
The most beautiful place is home.

# Chapter Three

One of the most important times in my life was when I formed the National Association For Health in the sixties.

When my brother Ronald became a Member of Parliament in 1935 he was the first Conservative Member to go down to Ebbw Vale.

He was horrified, not only by the sight of the extreme poverty being suffered there, but also by men dying in the street of starvation. The Prince of Wales had also been there and said that something must be done.

But nothing *was* done and my brother was so upset at it all that I started to help Lady Rees Williams, whose son was a Member of Parliament for South Kensington, in providing the women who were suffering from malnutrition and habitual abortion with Marmite. There were no vitamins in those days.

This was when I realized how important natural medicine could be in an emergency such as was happening in England at that time. They needed not only food but vegetables and fruit which of course they could not afford.

It was not until after World War II was over that I went to America for the first time and learnt about vitamins.

They told me when I arrived:

'We have something very new and very exciting which prevents one from suffering next morning if you had too much to drink last night. It also makes you feel extremely well. It is called Vitamin B.'

I was not drinking at night but I thought how many people needed help to feel active and well whatever they were doing.

I therefore not only took Vitamin B myself but brought it back for my family. Many people in England at that time were suffering from a vitamin deficiency although they were not aware of it.

The Vitamin B I had in America was, of course, synthetic. It was not until six years later in 1954 that natural medicine arrived in this country, near me at Hemel Hempstead, and I wrote a book called *Vitamins for Vitality*, which was a huge success.

Then, in 1964, realising how much it was needed, I started the National Association For Health and people laughed.

'You can get strawberries out of the freezer in January,' they said. 'What on earth do you want this for?'

I wish I could have told them that this was the beginning of a search for health which was to become one of the most important things of the century.

But at first people did not take me seriously.

It was not until 1978 that people who understood

what I was doing realised how important it was, and the first Helfex (Health Food Exhibition) was introduced to London.

By this time we had quite a number of people making the right vitamin capsules to eat and also providing excellent 'pick-me-ups' for people who felt tired and over-worked.

The best of these was called Bio-Strath which I heard of in Switzerland and I went out to see it being made.

Not only was it considered one of the best tonics for children but helped those whose brains were not particularly active. It was also marvellous for older people who were losing their balance. In fact, it was the only product of that sort on the market at that time. This was ignored or laughed at by the medical profession.

It was not until 1994 that the doctors admitted Bio-Strath was what I had always known it was, and they prescribed it for their patients.

To get back to 1978. The first Helfex took place. Maurice Hanssen, who was organising it, arranged for it to be at the Royal Lancaster Hotel in London, and I persuaded Earl Mountbatten to open it.

He was delighted to do so as he felt he was doing something which really helped people and was, of course, controversial, which was something he always enjoyed. He made an excellent speech, visited every different stall and naturally was photographed a thousand times.

The *Natural Food Retailer* magazine described it as 'a Right Royal Show'. Every year after that Helfex congregated all the Health Food Traders either at

Birmingham, Brighton, or other parts of England. Those coming from abroad to join us increased year by year.

After Helfex the Marquis of Bath had a special Fair for Honey at Longleat and asked me to open it.

I had always been very excited about honey because I believe it is a natural cure for many diseases.

It was Mohammed who said: 'Honey is not only the food of the body but also the food of the soul.'

It is in fact a natural food which is used by athletes because it makes them strong and able to run faster. At the same time it is a sedative for those who are mentally disturbed or suffering in an unusual manner.

When I first married my husband he had, when he was eighteen, been badly wounded at Passchendaele when a dum-dum bullet shot away his shoulder, as I have said. He was continually having the bullet pieces passing through his body and upsetting him. When that was happening it was very hard for him to sleep.

I gave him honey straight from the comb – and with the comb – twice a day and in a very short time he was entirely free from this very uncomfortable and upsetting occurrence.

It has been proved that if children are given honey, which is recommended to be put in their water instead of white sugar, they become, by the time they are seven, stronger and enjoy better health than other children.

Personally I drink honey every night and also in the morning. I do find it has an amazing effect on one's health. I wrote a book called *The Magic of Honey* which has been appreciated by people all over the world.

When we arrived at Longleat for the Honey Fair we found that it was laid out in the garden in a marquee. I went to each stall and found many different sorts of honey, all excellent in every way.

Everyone told me how thrilled they were to be able to breed bees and thus to have honey to give to people who really need it.

One had only to look at the people who had produced the honey to realise what a good effect it had on the complexion and strength of anyone who really believed in it.

As you can imagine I was very thrilled to see that honey was approved of by the Marquis. He was delighted to see us, and had the most romantic story of anyone I have known.

I had known him since the twenties. He had the most unusual and exciting marriage by having two weddings. He was an extremely handsome young man, whom I met when he was at Oxford. One of my best friends was his wife Daphne Vivian.

He asked her to marry him but his family disapproved of the idea and decided that he should go round the world to forget her. He was sent away but before he left they were married secretly and she wore her wedding ring on a chain round her neck. He went away for a year and came back and said he still wished to marry Daphne.

To the young couple's surprise the family gave in and they were married with much pomp and ceremony at St Paul's, Knightsbridge.

Raine at two months old. This was hailed as the most beautiful picture of a mother and daughter ever published.

Raine aged seven was reported to be the most photographed child in the country.

My great-grandmother came to England as an heiress and beauty from Philadelphia. Her grandfather, who was a close relative of the Duke of Hamilton, had to flee the country because he killed someone of importance in a duel.

I helped my beloved brother Ronald *(above left)* win the seat of Kings Norton in Birmingham for the Conservatives in 1935. When the War came, he joined the Worcestershire Yeomanry, in which his father had served and died. Ronald was killed at Dunkirk.

Ronald with the Prime Minister Winston Churchill *(above right)*, who rang my mother personally during Dunkirk, to see if Ronald was safe.

As the only lady Welfare Officer for Bedfordshire, I looked after 20,000 troops. Because many of them were on Secret Stations, to visit them I had to have a uniform. I became an Honorary member of the A.T.S.

I served the St. John Ambulance Brigade for fifty years.

On the day of the Royal Wedding I asked all the St. John people who had been on duty all night to come to Camfield to have something to eat and drink. While they were doing so, we watched the wedding on the television.

One of the famous photographs of me taken by Dorothy Wilding which is in all her exhibitions.

Singing with the Royal Philharmonic Orchestra when I was 77 years of age. I was the oldest woman ever to record her first album.

With Glen *(left)*, Hugh *(seated)* and Ian *(right)* soon after we arrived at
Camfield Place.

Katie Boyle *(top left)*, a great friend for many years; Prince Ranier of Monaco and his beautiful wife Grace Kelly *(top right)*; Zsa Zsa Gabor *(centre)*, a great star and a dear friend; Sir John Mills *(bottom left)*, who has starred in three of the films made of my books; Indira Gandhi *(bottom right)*, one of the first people I met when visiting India for the first time.

The Earl and Countess Mountbatten were two of my oldest and dearest friends and a very important part of my life.

The Duke and Duchess of Windsor.

I think I was one of the few people in the church who held their breath just in case someone announced they were already married and this ceremony was completely unnecessary. However, it passed without a single interruption.

They were very happy for quite a number of years. Not for ever, that would have been too much of a fairy story. But they had four children and I think Alexander, who was an adorable little boy, is a very unusual person today, but that is another story.

The Marquis was one of the many people who had now started to write to me on health.

Before the Recession the National Association For Health was valued at £600,000,000 with one-third going in export, and I received over 30,000 letters a year, from all over the world.

Of course it was very hard work getting people to realise as they do now, how good natural food is, especially for children.

I have always been extremely fortunate in having so many wonderful friends. I counted the Marquis of Bath as being one of the most charming and handsome of them.

Another of my very dear friends was Sir Arthur Bryant.

It was in 1980 that he was the Chairman at a Foyles Luncheon and I was the Guest of Honour.

Everyone who writes a book, especially if they want a lot of publicity for it, wants a Foyles luncheon.

I was the first person to receive a Foyles luncheon in their honour, a very long time ago. Christina Foyle was very young at the time and very nervous in case it was not a success.

It was in fact so successful that all through the years every author has tried to have a luncheon, which Christina makes particularly interesting because she chooses not only amusing books for the luncheon, but also amusing people to present them.

In 1980 the luncheon was not for one of my books but for *Laughter from a Cloud* by the Duchess of Marlborough. The Duchess's family did not support her and during her speech at the luncheon she said:

'Lord Charteris my Cousin is here, otherwise my family have really lost their sense of humour. They are nowhere to be seen.'

It was later that Sir Arthur Bryant wrote to tell me he was engaged to the Duchess of Marlborough whom he had met at the luncheon.

MYLES PLACE
THE CLOSE
SALISBURY

25th June 1980

Dearest Barbara,

I am writing to let you know before the surprise news is announced that Laura Marlborough and I are engaged to be married and that the announcement will be in *The Times* next week.

We fell in love at the Foyles Luncheon at which I had to take the chair, and only you will be able to understand how such a thing could have come about for such an unromantic looking object as myself.

But I love her dearly and as we have both been very lonely for a long time, I am very happy and can scarcely believe in such a, for me, wonderful piece of good fortune.

Yours affectionately,

Arthur

P.S. I have nearly finished *The Elizabethan Deliverance* and will be sending you the first copy that comes from the printer before it is published at Christmas. Your lovely little golden leaf from the tree she planted is on my hall table and is the first thing to catch the eye on entering my house.

I was delighted for Arthur's sake although I thought he might find the Duchess slightly overwhelming.

I sent Arthur one of the precious acorns from the tree which was planted in my garden by Elizabeth I when she was Princess Elizabeth and was a prisoner at Hatfield House.

However, in October that year the following appeared in the *Evening Standard:*

DISENGAGING TIMES FOR SIR ARTHUR AND LAURA

The remarkable engagement of Laura Duchess of Marlborough and historian Sir Arthur Bryant would seem to be off.

Sir Arthur, 81, has been telling friends that his fiancée has put an end to the match which was announced in June, a little over a month after they first met at the Foyles luncheon to launch her memoirs.

The couple who already have six marriages

between them certainly seem to be very sensitive about the subject when questioned.

When I rang Sir Arthur at his Salisbury home he refused to talk, although in the past he has always been most approachable and communicative.

The Duchess, 65, last wife of the last Duke of M. after being Viscountess Long, the Countess of Dudley and Mrs Michael Canfield, was scarcely more communicative when I contacted her holiday hotel in Portugal.

'There is nothing yet to put in the papers,' she said. When questioned further she abruptly terminated the conversation.

Perhaps more light on the matter will be shed when the Duchess returns from her holiday. On that day Sir Arthur Bryant will be chairing another Foyles lunch.


He did not marry for the third time.

I think perhaps he was very lonely when he was old but his books continued to be full of interest.

I always thought of him as one of the most charming as well as one of the most intelligent men I have ever met and I will miss him as long as I am alive.

He once said about my writing:

'I consider Barbara a good writer because she keeps to the point and never uses a superfluous word.' That is journalism, as Lord Beaverbrook taught me.

Arthur was our greatest historian whose books I have not only enjoyed but plagiarised continually for the background of my own novels.

In fact, I once said to him:

'I am always plagiarising you!' to which he replied:

'You know, as well as I do, that I am delighted for you to have the lot.'

I found his descriptions of the Battle of Trafalgar absolutely fascinating.

Also when I was writing my novel with Lord Mountbatten shortly before he was assassinated – *Love at the Helm* – I discovered through Arthur Bryant that the Americans who were plundering all the ships after our war with them had stopped, also pilfered a lot of the ships carrying food and other things to Wellington.

That reminds me of something that happened recently. It is often said that people are difficult in helping you. It is totally untrue, people always help me.

I rang up the War Office and asked if they would mind telling me what they paid the soldiers at the Battle of Waterloo.

They not only told me their pay, but told me how difficult it was to get the money through. Some men had to wait three months before they received their pay and they were not allowed to go home without it. They also told me what we paid Wellington.

I thought it was very kind, and I was so thrilled the other day when they had an exhibition of the wedding-dresses I had bought second-hand for the brides in the Services.

To get back to Foyles Luncheons: another was held for me in March 1990.

This time it was for the 'Royal' books which were

not a success. Although they had beautiful covers they were done too cheaply.

Actually the publishers, without consulting me, altered some of the things I put inside. I did not realise this until after the luncheon which was very enjoyable except a number of unexpected things happened.

I had asked the Duke of Argyll, who is a great friend of my sons, to be the Chairman.

He agreed and I deliberately did not ask his Step-mother, Margaret, the Duchess of Argyll, because I knew they did not get on well together.

The Press, however, thought they would be clever and persuaded the Duchess of Argyll to arrive uninvited and unseated to the luncheon.

She then tried to talk to the Duke who did not want to talk to her.

Because there was nowhere for her to sit Christina Foyle had to give up her seat.

Needless to say all this caused quite a sensation.

Naturally people were far more interested in the drama than in the reason why they had come to the luncheon.

I first saw Margaret Whigham (later Her Grace, The Duchess of Argyll) in 1931, dancing with my brother Ronald at a ball in Belgrave Square, given by Lord Monsell, who became The First Lord of the Admiralty.

She was outstandingly lovely and I asked who she was.

She sprang to fame that same year, after she was presented at Buckingham Palace to King George V and Queen Mary, a piece of pageantry which I enjoyed twice myself and find it exceedingly sad that it no longer takes place.

Margaret was undoubtedly the most beautiful debutante of the year. She had a sweet, gentle nature, besides being really lovely and was to start the vogue of publicity for debutantes. Every succeeding year every girl hoped to emulate Margaret's news value which swept her into the forefront of all gossip columns.

Young married women had in the twenties been the most publicised members of society and although an eye had been kept on the girls, 'as one never knew who they might marry', they were not news from the point of view of being debutantes.

Margaret changed this.

Debutantes' points were discussed and speculated upon before they made their debut, then when the Season started there was a frantic newspaper search for the favourite.

Margaret gave a more flattering Press Conference than any film star.

After she married the Duke of Argyll she took part in a pageant, 'Famous Beauties Down the Ages', which was by invitation only and 500 of my daughter's guests paid five guineas each to watch it.

The Duchess of Argyll, as Margaret was then, was reported as being a ravishingly lovely Marie Antoinette, wearing a diamond necklace which had actually belonged to the unhappy Queen, which she had borrowed for the occasion from the Duchess of Sutherland.

There was a cabaret for which I produced and wrote the script and lyrics: something called *The Debutante's Dilemma* was performed by the most glamorous debutantes of the year. The lyrics were cynical – a new attitude which was just coming 'in' on television.

Margaret went on being the great beauty of the age until her marriage broke up and she concentrated on her poodle dogs which went with her everywhere. When the Duke died she sold her house in Grosvenor Street and moved into an hotel.

She was surrounded by a collection of devoted women friends, and her precious dogs which she loved she said 'more than anyone else'! In fact, when one died she wept bitterly and it took a long time to comfort her.

She had a long battle with the Duke of Argyll, her Stepson, who had taken his Father's place, but as she grew older still, she found a consolation in imagining in the Nursing Home where she was staying that she was travelling around the world in a ship.

I shall always remember her, however, as one of the most beautiful young girls I have ever seen, who brought about a new attitude from the Press towards debutantes.

Another of my dear friends was Indira Gandhi for whom I had tremendous regard and admiration ever since I met her when she was very young.

As Prime Minister she was now going through the same difficulties with her country as we have been going through recently with ours.

Here is the letter I received from her explaining the situation:

Prime Minister's House
New Delhi
September 20 1981

Dear Barbara Cartland,

This is the first time when there has been such a delay in thanking you for your packet of vitamins, creams and book. This is not because of lack of appreciation but lack of time.

As the world situation becomes more and more complex, financial and other burdens bear down more heavily on those who occupy positions of responsibility. One feels a bit like Alice's Queen running faster and faster but not really getting anywhere.

There is one point which I have wanted to clarify for some time. About a couple of months or so ago I saw an article which stated that my Government regarded Dickie Mountbatten as *persona non grata* and, according to the article, when this was conveyed to him by someone, he replied that he could not abide a Police State. I wish this article had appeared in Dickie's lifetime or that I had known that such ridiculous stories were being circulated. Needless to say, there is absolutely no truth in this. We have never considered him as anything but a good friend of the family and of India. In fact whenever he has asked something I have gone out of my way to try and accommodate him somehow. Not only I but Indian people hold him in high regard. Also, in spite of and during Emergency, we have not had anything like a Police State in India at any time. During the emergency some people were arrested, some were politicians but the larger number were what we call anti-social elements – smugglers, dacoits, hoarders, black-marketeers etc., whose activities had been pushing up our prices, creating shortages and were generally harmful to the people as a whole. Not once during emergency was there any show of police strength. We ourselves had released all political prisoners some time before the 1977 elections. When the Janata Party came to power, it released the criminals, with dire consequences from which we have not yet recovered. When we were re-elected in 1980, the people wanted us to have some sort of emergency again and I am now being blamed for softness.

I did not mean this letter to be so long but I did want to clear the point about Dickie. I hope his family does not hold similar views. It is possible that my dear Aunt, who was very friendly with them all but who has disliked me since I was a little girl, may have spread such stories. Unfortunately she is in the habit of doing so not only about those whom she does not approve of but even about her friends.

There is a possibility of my coming to London in March 1982 for the Festival of India. Heaven knows what the world will be like by then. I may also stop over for just a few hours to break journey when I return from the Mexico Conference back to Delhi.

With good wishes

Indira Gandhi

It was when *This Is Your Life* was given for me for the second time that I met many more of my friends.

On November 8th 1989 I was asked to go to one of the studios in Elstree to talk about a film of mine which was being rehearsed there.

When I arrived, to my surprise, Michael Aspel turned up in a horse-drawn carriage and jumping out said: 'Barbara Cartland *This Is Your Life*.'

It was the last thing I was expecting but of course I was delighted when I realised I was to be the first person who had ever been the subject of *This Is Your Life* twice.

The first one had been in March 1958 with Eamonn Andrews.

The second programme eventually took place at the Studios in Teddington.

We were delayed because Margaret, Duchess of Argyll, who was to take part, arrived twenty minutes late and demanded that her poodle be fed immediately with the best chicken.

This took some time but at last we took our places on the set.

I came on with Michael Aspel, wearing a pink sequined gown designed by Norman Hartnell.

Everything went quite smoothly until they asked the Duchess of Argyll a question and she completely dried up.

I realised what had happened and burst into an eulogy of how beautiful she had been when I had first seen her as a debutante in the early thirties dancing with my brother.

Thames Television had taken a great deal of trouble to bring in people I had not expected, including a couple who had been married for forty years.

Their marriage was happy, the wife said, due to the fact that when she was in the Auxiliary Territorial Service (A.T.S.) during the war I had provided her with a white wedding-dress which her husband had admired very much.

Actually to tell you the whole story it did not start with the wedding-dresses.

I have always tried to help other people and one of the most challenging ideas I have ever thought of occurred to me during World War II.

It was to dress the Service women for their weddings.

When war came my husband and I left our large house in Grosvenor Square, and moved with our three children to a small four-hundred-year-old thatched cottage which my husband and I had bought to be alone at weekends if we wanted to be.

It was on the river at Great Barford in Bedfordshire, and was very attractive. But it was a squeeze to get us all into it. The children, however, adored the garden and the river beyond it.

I soon found myself first of all working for the W.V.S. (Women's Voluntary Service), and soon I was giving out all the books for the Searchlight batteries for their recreation time. I then became the only lady Welfare Officer for Bedfordshire.

As it was in the centre of England it contained most of the secret stations and I therefore had to have a uniform to get into them.

I was made an Honorary member of the A.T.S. 'Honorary' meaning that I was not paid and I could give in my notice if everyone annoyed me!

The first thing I realised was that the women working at making balloons in Cardington in Bedfordshire, and at other places, were bored because they did not feel they were really in the War, as they never heard a shot fired in anger.

Consequently some of them went on leave and did not come back, and they were altogether 'on edge'.

At the time the great fashion was 'cami-knickers' and I went to Peter Jones where I managed to buy the most beautiful material, very cheaply, without coupons, for them to make themselves cami-knickers.

They measured the material, and cut them out on the floor of the Welfare Office and a senior officer said:

'It will certainly improve morale, if not morals!'

The women then came to me and said:

'We cannot be married in our hideous uniforms, when we want to be in white.'

So I plucked up courage and went to the War Office to ask if we could have extra coupons with which to buy their wedding-gowns.

I was eyed somewhat severely by the women generals, because it had already gone round that someone had said to me:

'I hear you call all the Generals "Darling".'

To which I had replied:

'Only the men!'

When I asked about the extra coupons one of the women generals said:

'Don't you know there is a war on?'

With trepidation I said that I did, but if they could

not give me coupons, I might be able to get the wedding-gowns second-hand.

An elderly woman, looking very fierce and general-like said:

'Mrs McCorquodale must have a trusting faith in human nature.'

I felt so angry at their lack of understanding for the women who felt that a wedding day was the most important day of their lives, that I went home and advertised in *The Lady*.

My advertisement was answered and I bought two wedding-dresses, complete with veils, one for £7 and one for £8.

I paid for them myself and sent them to the War Office with my compliments.

They then did an 'about turn' and said they would have a 'Pool of Wedding Dresses' which the brides could borrow for £1 a day but I had to provide them!

I found that buying wedding-dresses was not half as difficult as they had thought. After advertising I went round locally to poor houses with several children scrambling on the floor, and a very harassed mother, trying to cope.

She would open a drawer and there, in tissue paper, was a wedding-dress she had only worn once, which in those days had cost about £15. Unless they were marked underneath the arms, they were perfect.

By the end of the war I had bought one thousand wedding-dresses and sent to them to the War Office.

My maid, however, who had pressed them and removed any little marks from them before they were dispatched, said to me firmly:

'One thing I am quite certain of. If I get married, it will not be in white!'

To return to my story of the programme, a wonderful tribute was paid to me by Lady Pamela Hicks, who was looking very pretty. She was Lord Mountbatten's second daughter, and she said that my vitamins had helped her Father enormously.

My daughter Raine, and her husband, as they were unable to reach the Studio, did a very good 'turn' from Althorp.

They were sitting side by side and were an extremely handsome couple.

There is no doubt at all that Raine made Johnnie so very happy in his life and he was so different in every way from what he had been when they were first married.

He had been, I always thought, slightly aloof from the world and not a part of it. But Raine made him realise how much Althorp had to give to the people and how the right atmosphere was one of love and help for all people from every part of the world.

That was what changed Johnnie in many ways, so that he was in fact, through his second marriage, not only a happier man, but a much more charming and delightful man for other people to meet.

I think that never before had he been encouraged to mix with the many people who came to visit the house as an ancestral home and paid their money to look round.

What he gave them was a new idea of the Squire, in the full sense of the word, and he sent them away with the memory of what he had said to them and how charming he could be, as an ordinary man rather than the owner of a great estate.

When they made my film, *A Duel of Hearts* at Althorp in 1990, there was no doubt at all that the star of that incident was Beryl Reid.

Beryl Reid was always a great person for being amused. When she was first brought down to Camfield by a friend to meet me at dinner, she sat down, enjoyed her dinner, but afterwards said:

'I am not leaving until I have been insulted! I have always been told that when you come here you feel insulted by something the hostess has said!'

I did not think it was very funny at the time but I realised afterwards that it was the sort of way Beryl always talked and made herself known.

She was terribly good in *A Duel of Hearts* and she undoubtedly has always been one of the great comediennes on the British stage.

Prince Alexis, who is one of my French publishers, came over specially from Paris for *This Is Your Life*.

Dear John Mills, whom I have known and loved for over forty years, spoke about me and my films.

I met him first when I became interested in health, because he says that the reason he has been able to act at his advanced age, has been due to the fact that he always follows The Hay Diet.

This is the diet when one does not mix protein and carbohydrates at the same meal, which allows the stomach to digest the food properly. By observing this method of eating one does not put on weight.

I have often visited him at his charming house in Denham, which is typical of him, because it is so attractive. At the same time it vibrates with all his enthusiasm, which he has never lost. In fact, he is most enthusiastic towards life which so many older people are unable to be.

I had a charming afternoon at Brocket Hall when John Mills and Helen Hayes, whom I have known for years, were filming Agatha Christie's *The Mirror Crack'd*.

I had tea with all the members of the cast and found them as fascinating off the stage as they were on.

John Mills is a real example of a great actor who never forgets his part as a leading man, and he will definitely lead until he is no longer with us.

*This Is Your Life* also had a little of me singing 'A Nightingale Sang in Berkeley Square', which I had sung with the Royal Philharmonic Orchestra in 1978.

Archie Newman, who ran the orchestra, had rung me up and said:

'I want to do the love songs of the twenties, and thirties and no one will remember them as well as you. Will you give me a list?'

Of course I said I would. But the songs which we danced to remained in our minds because the lyrics were so good.

There was a pause before Archie said:

'Well there is no reason why we should not have singers.'

'That would make it much better,' I replied. 'And I am sure the words are what people remember more than the music.'

It was while Glen and I were motoring in Guadalupe, having had a very good luncheon at some wayside hotel, that I said to Glen:

'I have an idea. When I first came to London there was a man called Whispering Jack Smith who used to whisper at the night clubs. He produced a marvellous sound which we all enjoyed and which we danced to.'

Glen was listening but like most sons he is not particularly interested in one's past.

'I have just thought,' I said, 'that I might sing with the Royal Philharmonic Orchestra.'

'Mummy, you must be mad!' he said.

Although I did not talk about it again to Glen, when I came home I saw Archie Newman and said:

'I have got a beautiful list for you but of course I would like to sing them myself.'

He looked at me in astonishment.

'Do you sing?' he asked.

'I used to, back in the twenties,' I replied. 'In fact I sang in one charity show with Douglas Byng, when he was dressed up as my Mother. I sang: "Why Don't the Men Propose, Mama?" Everyone said at the time that I sang very well.'

'Well then, why not?' Archie said. 'If you can sing there is no reason why you should not sing the songs you have suggested to me.'

I was thrilled at the idea.

I got hold of a friend of mine called Peter Hallam who trained two local orchestras. At first I merely asked him if it was possible for me to sing at my age.

He gave me a song to sing which was, and still is, my favourite – 'A Nightingale Sang in Berkeley Square.'

I joined him at the piano and when I had finished he said:

'Marvellous! Absolutely marvellous! I should think you sang that in exactly the same way as you did when you were twenty!'

I told Archie what I was doing. He was still enthusiastic about it and said:

'Do not worry. We have things these days which can make your voice sound the same as when you were eighteen.'

It became one of the most exciting things I did in that year.

Of course I practised very hard with Peter and became, at the age of seventy-seven, the oldest woman ever to record her first *Album of Love Songs*. In fact, the cassette became a present I gave to my friends.

The Earl Mountbatten of Burma always played it when he was alone at breakfast. Jean Rook used to play it in her car when she was driving to work. She said my 'pure little virgin voice' inspired her for the whole day.

Although I was said to be singing with the Royal Philharmonic Orchestra, I actually did my singing in an E.M.I. Studio, and Norman Newell, who is an old and dear friend, produced me.

He gave me an instrument which looked rather like a sponge into which I sang, and said:

'It is very, very sensitive! If you even raise your chin it makes a sound. With this microphone you need not force your voice at all.'

I sang extremely quietly, but it came out, as everybody said, exactly right on the songs.

Apart from my favourite, I liked 'How Much Do I Love You?' One song particularly moved me almost to tears, and that was 'I'll See You Again' because it reminded me of Ronald.

They allowed me to say in the middle of it the poem I had particularly written about him:

### Those Hours Are Mine

I am so happy that we had those days,
　　Wind in our faces, and a cloudless sky.
I am so happy that we had those nights,
　　Do you remember how the moonlight made
　　　you sigh?
Every note I hear, each shaft of sun,
　　Reminds me of something we have done.
Music which echoes down the years,
　　Music of laughter with a touch of tears.
Your hand in mine, the times we talked together,
　　Those hours are mine, for ever and for ever.

Then I sang the last words of 'I'll See You Again' which are:

　　　. . . Though my world may go awry,
　　　In my heart will ever lie
　　　Just the echo of a sigh – goodbye!

When it came to the word 'goodbye' my voice genuinely broke. Archie and everyone were delighted because it sounded so moving. While I was slightly embarrassed, all those who heard it said that it was excellent and exactly what they wanted.

At the end of *This Is Your Life* everyone walked to the front of the stage, with my Grandson's wife Victoria carrying my Great-Granddaughter Claudia

in her arms, while my Great-Grandson Edward, aged
three, ran to me, and seizing the pink sequins of my
gown, kept saying:

'Pretty dress! Pretty dress!'

No one could have had a higher compliment from
a young man.

After it had ended I realised that it was quite easy
for me to reach up to the first row of the audience
where there were the old people who had been
watching all the time.

I stretched up and shook them by the hand.

Afterwards the 'warm-up comedian' came up to
me and said I was the first person of all the *This Is
Your Life* programmes they had ever done, to take
any notice or shake hands with the members of the
public.

I thought this was extraordinary as the audience
on those occasions are nearly all elderly people who
come a long distance because they consider it an
outing for them.

Thames Television then supplied us with a
delicious supper and plenty to drink. It was a very
exciting evening for me.

One thing which did occur that evening and which
could have been a disaster was when I walked
towards the audience. There was a gap in the stage
which housed the cameras and as I walked forward
I almost fell into this opening. Even now I do not
know how I managed to avoid it.

There are many people for whom I have had great
admiration throughout my life, and someone I
admire more than anyone else and whom I have

known for so many years is Margaret Thatcher.

When I first came to Camfield I often spoke for her as she was in a constituency next door. We used to meet at the Alexandra Palace which was later burnt down.

I was quite certain then, because she was one of the few women who understood about money, that if we were ever to have a woman Prime Minister, she would be the one. She had learnt early in life to understand the variations and difficulties of money and therefore could handle it as no other woman was capable of doing.

It was in November 1989 that I asked her to come to luncheon with her husband to meet people in the County.

We had a very nice luncheon party with twelve detectives scouring the garden beforehand and looking under every blade of grass. Another six detectives arrived with the Prime Minister and her husband. Afterwards she wrote me a letter in which she said how much she had enjoyed the luncheon party.

When the new Prime Minister, John Major, came into office I also asked him to luncheon to meet some of the people of the County. When he and his wife accepted, I was delighted.

I was, however, astonished when he first walked into the house as I had no idea he was so tall. I had only seen him on the television when he always appears quite short. Instead of which a man of over 6ft walked into the hall. For a moment I thought the wrong person had come to luncheon.

He was very interesting and helpful in all he said.

We had a long talk about how we could get back to some form of morality. It was he, not I as the Press later said, who invented the idea of 'Back to Basics' but we did discuss it. '

I told him, which of course he knew, that the last Prime Minister, Margaret Thatcher, had said that we must get back to morality. It was easier said than done, which the Prime Minister understood.

He was a great success because one of my guests – who is always good value in any party – argued with him at luncheon.

The Prime Minister really got quite heated over the argument, moving his arms in the air and speaking out in a very authoritative manner.

Everyone said to me afterwards: 'Why does he not do that in the House of Commons?'

It was marvellous and we were all terribly impressed.

My sons were delighted with Norma, whom they found very, very attractive. She was absolutely charming and everybody who had not met her before, said how delightful she was.

When they drove away, the Prime Minister had four detectives, with the other twelve, who were local, waving them goodbye.

Norma followed in a car driving herself. I could not help thinking that they might have let one of the detectives go with her.

I have been in correspondence with the Prime Minister ever since, and in my opinion he is improving day by day, and getting more and more firm and authoritative.

As I listened to him in May 1994 on the television –

and I sent him a message the next morning – he is saying exactly the things we want to hear from him. He will, if he is given the chance, become, in his own way, a great Prime Minister.

But I was delighted to be able to write to him recently and say that Russia had signed a contract for my books in very large numbers. Up to now my books had always been plagiarised in a big way. But now the signed contract gives them twenty-four books a year with 125,000 copies of each, amounting to three million of my books.

What I heard at the same time is that in China, every book from Europe is having all the sex taken out. It seems to me they will only have a few pages left to print. The only books which are not interfered with are mine.

The Japanese who bought a lot of my books are so thrilled with them that they are thinking of treating other books in the same way as the Chinese.

Of course what people do not realise is that the reason I sell so much East of Suez is because it is in the contract of every marriage that a man has a virgin wife.

I have said so often to young people and I will say it again that I have been all over the world and I have never met a man of any class, creed, colour or nationality who wants us to go into a room with his wife and the mother of his children and wonder how many other men have been to bed with her.

It has now been proved in England, and these are not my statistics, that if you live with a man before you marry him, the marriage, on average, lasts only three years.

I was very surprised recently when I went to Germany.

I said to the Germans:

'We are very upset in England that one in two marriages fail which of course affects the children more than anything else. That is fifty per cent of the whole.'

They said in Germany it was sixty per cent.

I really thought that German women particularly would sit at home with their children which unfortunately in England we have ceased to do for a long time, due to Women's Lib.

When I am at home, one of the things I most enjoy is having luncheon parties on a Sunday, with my family.

I invite interesting people, and one of the most exciting I have had recently is Buddy Greco, the most famous singing pianist in the whole of America.

When he came over to England in 1993, he said that the one person he wanted to meet was me. So I gave a special luncheon for him at Camfield.

He arrived with a very pretty girl, Susie Anders, who works with him. The conversation was very amusing and bright and then suddenly Buddy took my hand in his and started to sing his favourite song which was: 'When I Fall In Love, It Will Be For Ever'.

He sang it so beautifully that everybody felt the tears coming into their eyes.

When he returned home he said that of all the people he had met in Europe, I was the one person he had enjoyed meeting most. He indicated that he would be dedicating his new album to me, because he had been so inspired by our meeting.

The famous film star Linda Christian, who was once married to Tyrone Power, came to luncheon with me a short time ago, and I found her enchanting.

We had a wonderful time together, talking over past memories.

I was delighted to hear what Linda had said about me recently in an interview on American television:

'I suppose the highlight of my visit to London was surely meeting Barbara Cartland for the first time. I have met every great movie star since the 1950s. As a personality Barbara surpasses them all. When Barbara enters a room every woman seems to fade into insignificance. It is because she has such an arresting and luminous personality. Coupled with her incredible achievements as the world's best selling author for me, and thousands of other people, Barbara Cartland must be voted "The Woman of This Century".'

One person I find extremely interesting is a young astrologer, who is the first one who has ever been taken by a stock exchange to tell them the way of the stars.

Guy Francis went to Hong Kong to do this, and was such a success that the Japanese persuaded him to go on to Japan. He reads my stars for me every year, and so far has been completely correct in everything he has told me.

It is, although people laugh, a tremendous help to know what is going to happen and to avoid the difficult consequences before they actually arrive.

I have been not only very fortunate in knowing Guy Francis who is a magnificent guide to the stars but also in finding Graham Wyley, the greatest expert on ghosts in this country – and possibly in the world – and his wife. They are both also outstanding healers.

Graham Wyley is collecting information on ghosts from every country to make a magnificent film of them.

He has removed the ghosts from my house, from Lord Brocket's – a crying child which upset them all – and has performed the same service in a great number of other famous houses as well.

He discovered in Windsor Castle the tunnel which was created by Charles II so that he could reach Nell Gwynn in the house outside the castle, and found it very creepy and strange.

On one occasion I had met a man in America who was in great pain from a broken rib. Graham, in England at the time, was able to stop his suffering, even at that great distance.

Graham's wife Thelma, who is very attractive, is so original in the way she helps animals. If one telephones her about a horse or a dog she can cure it, without even seeing it.

I have sent them so many different people recently and each time they have been successful, just by thought and not by touch, something on which most healers insist.

One of my friends who is also very talented is Sheikha Shenda, who is one of the foremost sculptresses.

She has sculpted a great number of people including, just recently, our present Prime Minister, John Major, and King Husain of Jordan and Queen Noor.

She is also completing a very large waterfall for a children's zoo.

Her husband, who is very interesting, comes originally from Iran and is really the only man who is entitled lawfully to call himself a sheikh, although he has lived in England now for a long time.

They are an enchanting couple who have a Georgian house on the Embankment, where they give the most amusing and delightful luncheons, and a house in Cambridgeshire where there are a great number of large statues.

I have written in an earlier book of an extraordinary party I attended at Deauville in 1923 where the host was Sir James Dunn who had asked me to marry him.

The party included someone else for whom I had great admiration and that was Lady Diana Cooper. She was there together with her husband and twenty-four other people.

I was only allowed to go if I was chaperoned so I took with me my greatest friend the Marchioness of Queensberry.

It was an extraordinary party in which I quarrelled with an unknown young man called Noël Coward. But we later made it up and became great friends.

Lady Diana Cooper was one of the most beautiful women of the century. It was not only her pale facial skin, like delicate eggshell porcelain, her translucent blue eyes and pale gold hair. It was also because she was not content to be a beautiful face.

She had always been in the headlines doing something new. In 1919 she fell through a skylight watching the fireworks in Peace-week; she was the first person I ever heard of to use black sheets; she played the lead in *The Miracle* in New York and England, in which she had to stand motionless for forty minutes.

She married the man she loved although he had no money and worked in his constituency for him, as no woman had ever worked before, to get him elected to Parliament.

She opened a flower shop; she and her butler sold the shingle from the shore in front of her house at Bognor Regis; she raised pigs; and she became the most beautiful Ambassadress we have ever had in Paris!

I am always convinced she saved my life when during a storm she insisted on a yacht on which we were travelling to Deauville in 1923 turning round and returning to Southampton.

She had so many extraordinary and fascinating facets to her character. She was, in fact, the first woman to drive her own private car.

Lady Diana Cooper was amusing, witty, frank and unselfconscious. She had a sympathy and understanding with the young, the middle-aged and she old.

That is real beauty inside and out!

# Chapter Four

Now I am so old I find myself looking back at the glamour and the pageantry of England of which so much has unfortunately been lost.

This worries me because never again will we be able to show foreigners and ourselves the pageantry of the Royal Family which was so outstanding and greatly envied by everyone on the Continent.

It is also rather sad that very few people give private Balls today, and we have to rely on the Balls for charity which are attended by the Royal Family, to have any of the glamour which existed in the past.

The amazing Fancy Dress Ball given at Devonshire House by Her Grace The Duchess of Devonshire in 1897 has gone down into history as the most magnificent occasion on which even Edward Prince of Wales and his beautiful wife Alexandra dressed up.

What we have lost, which I regret more than anything else, are the Presentations of the debutantes at the Drawing Rooms at Buckingham Palace which existed until they were swept away by Edward VIII in the short time before his Abdication.

I was presented some time after I became a debutante as my Mother, who had been so devastated by my Father being killed after four years in the trenches in 1918, had not felt like doing anything social.

However, in 1925 she agreed that I must be Presented and I was thrilled from the very moment I sat in The Mall with three white Prince of Wales' Feathers in my hair, and wearing a gown covered in silver sequins made for me as advertisement by a young Cambridge undergraduate called Norman Hartnell, who had just opened a shop in Bruton Street.

I brought him his first customers and my dress was the forerunner of the marvellous creations that were to be worn later by Queen Elizabeth (now Queen Mother) and her daughter Queen Elizabeth II for whom he designed her Coronation Gown.

As I sat in The Mall, with sightseers peering through the car windows, it seemed a long wait.

Courts were very large after the War, with 700 or 800 Presentations being the average, and it was well known that King George and Queen Mary used to rest in the afternoon before one took place.

When I got into Buckingham Palace I went up the stairs on which the Gentlemen-At-Arms stood on every alternate step.

I went into the huge red, white and gold Ballroom on the first floor, which was often incorrectly called 'The Throne Room'.

Only a very small percentage of those present could get a seat on the rows of narrow, scarlet-covered benches. Latecomers waited in an ante-room on gilt chairs, which had a concert-hall atmosphere.

The Court began with the wives of the Foreign Ambassadors and Ministers making the official presentations in the Diplomatic Circle, during which the King and Queen remained standing.

Then a long, perfectly-regulated procession of debutantes filed by, each preceded by her mother or whoever presented her. Two curtsies were made, one to the King and one to the Queen.

Queen Mary's rope upon rope of pearls were sensational and the Diplomats in their gold-covered uniforms rivalled the women, the married ones of whom wore tiaras.

The Lord Chamberlain called out my Mother's name and then mine. I curtsied first to H.M. King George V and then to H.M. Queen Mary.

As I moved away my train was picked up by an aide-de-camp and thrown over my arm.

I was then free to wander about, to eat fruit salad, sandwiches and fruit cake, supplied by Lyons, and served by powdered footmen in the Royal Livery.

When the last Presentation was over the Band struck up 'God Save The King'. The Court Officials and Officers of State led the Royal Procession, walking backwards.

The King and Queen, who had risen from their thrones, turned to the right, to the left and then to the centre. The King made three bows and the Queen three curtsies to the assembled company.

Then Queen Mary placed her hand in the King's and he led her from the throne, to wave upon wave of curtsying women.

A lovely sight, magnificent, yet simple in its dignity as only British pageantry can be.

I remember feeling very near to tears.

I want to tell you a funny story, although it is rather unkind, about a painting of the Drawing Room at Buckingham Palace.

When I was writing my book *Barbara Cartland's Celebrities* in 1982, I particularly wanted to write an article about the Drawing Room at Buckingham Palace and I remembered there had been a picture of it painted by a famous artist.

I rang up Buckingham Palace and said:

'Will you please tell me if you have the painting named "A Drawing Room"?'

'The Drawing Room has never been painted,' they said.

'Oh yes it has,' I replied.

They then produced an old fellow who was rather doddery who said:

'There's never been a picture of it in my time.'

But I knew there was.

Then I remembered that upstairs in my house I had a number of *Tatlers*. I had written for them for three years under a pseudonym, and was also the Social Editoress.

When the editor, Hutchinson left, for some unknown reason they burnt all the *Tatlers*.

I fortunately had kept twenty-four of them at home. I looked through them and there was the picture I wanted.

It was painted by Sir John Lavery.

Unfortunately it does not show the time I was presented but it was painted three years later when

Margaret Whigham (later the Duchess of Argyll) and various other people I knew were presented. It had been beautifully painted and was in the centre of the *Tatler*.

I rang up Buckingham Palace and said:

'Oh, by the way, I have discovered who did the painting and I would love to know where it is.'

'Well we have not got it,' was the reply.

End of conversation!


Over the years Buckingham Palace has seen many events which have changed the course of history.

On April 24th 1986 it was reported in the newspapers that the Duchess of Windsor had died.

It seemed to me extraordinary at that time, as it had before, that one woman of no great importance from America should have turned topsy-turvy the Royal Family of Great Britain.

I found an old letter when my Mother died, written to her in 1918 in which I said:


... I went to a wonderful *Thé Dansant* at the Kerr-Smileys on Sunday.

It was one of the best they have given.

Ernest took me home in a taxi and tried to kiss me.

Such cheek! Of course I refused to let him.


Ernest was the brother of Mrs. Kerr-Smiley who had a large house in Belgrave Square.

She was very firm to me and all the debutantes in saying:

'It is no use you girls looking at Ernest because he has to marry money!'

We laughed at this. But Ernest did not marry 'money'.

He went to America and came back about ten years later with his second wife and I was asked to meet her at a luncheon party the day she arrived.

Ernest had always seemed rather a reserved man, so I was very anxious to see what sort of wife he had chosen.

When I was introduced to Wallis Warfield I was frankly disappointed.

She wore a dowdy black dress and a shapeless hat which accentuated her very bad complexion. She had large hands and used them too much. She was, however, very vivacious, but was too obviously determined to be aggressively American.

She had brought with her to the luncheon, attended by all women, half-a-dozen handkerchiefs which were printed with pictures and bawdy parodies of nursery rhymes. The other women present laughed, but I thought it was in bad taste and it was not my type of humour.

In the next few years I began to see and hear a lot about the Simpsons. They were often at the famous Embassy Club on a Thursday night and at other clubs. I never went to a theatre without finding them in the stalls.

Wallis became smarter and she had her complexion improved miraculously by a face massage given to her by a Canadian. She was also becoming more charming and developed a natural gaiety which made everything she said sound witty.

I did, however, feel sad when I learnt from a nurse who had attended me, that she had been with Wallis Simpson when she had an operation to prevent her from having any children. It was fashionable at the time and was known as 'having one's ovaries tied'.

I thought Ernest, who had always been so English, would, like most Englishmen, want at least one son to follow in his footsteps and bear his name.

But when I had luncheon with Wallis in her flat at Bryanston Square I saw that it was no place for children.

I had a great friend, Thelma, Lady Furness, who was the twin of Gloria Vanderbilt, and very beautiful.

Thelma had surplanted Freda Dudley Ward in the affections of the Prince of Wales. Because Thelma was American she took up with the Simpsons and Wallis became her closest friend, so they moved in the Prince's Circle.

Thelma was a charming person, intelligent, beautiful and kind and everyone thought she gave the Prince a happiness he had not known before.

She was discreet about her position and the most critical of court officials admitted that she was 'no trouble'.

Wallis began to get grand.

In 1934 I was walking with a friend in Park Lane when I met Thelma.

'I am off to America,' she told us.

'The Prince will not like that,' my friend said. 'What will he do without you?'

Thelma smiled.

'I have asked Wallis to look after the "little man". He will be safe with her.'

She walked on.

'Wallis may not be beautiful,' I said reflectively. 'But I think nowadays she has become definitely fascinating.'

Those who knew the Prince of Wales well and were his closest friends, were aware that he was very nervous and shy. His love affairs were never as completely satisfying as they should have been.

Thelma said to me once:

'He is a great trier!'

The Prince of Wales made it very clear that he was miserable at Thelma leaving him.

Thelma set off for America and aboard the ship was the most talked about man in London, Aly Khan. Prince Aly Khan, son of the Aga Khan, was a very dashing, handsome man whom practically all women found irresistible.

It was a well-known story that he had, at one time, three women staying at the Ritz Hotel at the same time. He went from one bedroom to the other without any of them realising there was anyone else there with him.

Aly Khan lost no time in making Thelma aware of how lucky they were to be aboard the ship together.

The cables from the Prince were pathetic. But he was far away and Aly Khan was on the spot.

They danced. He never left her side.

From the moment she arrived in New York there were huge bouquets of flowers arriving every morning with notes saying when he expected to meet her.

Just as they had done on board ship, they dined together, they talked, they danced.

When Thelma sailed for England – something she

had delayed longer than she should have done – she was surprised to find that her cabin was almost filled with roses. There were roses on the chest-of-drawers, roses against the walls, roses on the floor.

It was when everyone who had come to say 'good-bye' had gone ashore that the telephone rang.

'Hello, darling,' a voice said. 'It is Aly. Will you have luncheon with me today?'

Thelma thought it was some sort of joke.

But – what a surprise? – he was on the ship and travelling back to England with her.

As had been arranged before she went to America Thelma drove down in the afternoon to Fort Belvedere to be with the Prince.

She found Wallis was also a guest.

Thelma had a bad cold when she arrived, and she went to bed early that night, hoping it would be better in the morning.

It was after dinner on Saturday that she noticed the Prince and Wallis seeming to have little private jokes.

As he picked up a piece of lettuce in his fingers Wallis playfully slapped his hand.

Thelma caught her eye and shook her head.

She thought that Wallis knew, as well as anybody else, that the Prince could be very friendly but, no matter how friendly, he never permitted familiarity.

As she wrote: 'His image of himself was shy, genial and democratic, but always framed by the Three Royal Feathers.'

To Thelma's astonishment Wallis looked straight at her.

It was then she realised why the Prince had seemed strange since she had returned from America.

Wallis, of all people!

She wrote: 'This was the friend I had asked jokingly to look after the Prince while I was away. The friend to whom I had gone for advice, and who assured me that the "little man" had missed me very much.'

Thelma knew then that Wallis had looked after him 'exceedingly well'.

That one cold, defiant glance told her the whole story.

Thelma left Fort Belvedere the following morning.

In a short time there was no doubt, as the whisperings grew and grew, that the tales about Wallis and the Prince of Wales were true.

It was not until January of 1936 that grave concern was expressed over the health of His Majesty the King.

The Prince was flown to Sandringham at the request of the Queen and it was from there that he telephoned Wallis to say that the King was dying.

Lord Dawson, the King's physician gave out the famous bulletin:

'The King's life is moving peacefully to its close.'

The Prince of Wales was now His Majesty King Edward VIII.

He surprised Godfrey Thomas, his Private Secretary, by saying that he wanted to see himself proclaimed King at St. James's Palace. He was accompanied by Wallis, and the National Anthem was played. They were both very moved.

'Wallis,' the Prince told her, 'there will be a difference, of course. But nothing can ever change my feelings towards you.'

The Prince had insisted, against everyone's advice, that the whole funeral Procession, with the exception of the Ladies of the Royal Family, should march on foot to Paddington Station. It was from there that the coffin was to travel by train for the internment at Windsor.

As they passed me, I heard a man remark:

'Lord Beatty looks ill. He will never get to Paddington.'

Admiral of the Fleet, Lord Beatty, was one of the many who collapsed on that long Procession, and he died shortly afterwards.

As the King walked behind his Father's coffin, the sapphire and diamond Maltese Cross from the top of the Imperial Crown broke off and rolled on the ground.

A Sergeant-Major retrieved it as the King exclaimed:

'Christ! What is going to happen next!'

It was learnt later that Ernest Simpson had gone to America and Wallis was intending to divorce him. A Divorce Petition was put down for hearing at the Ipswich Assizes.

The American Press was full of predictions that she would marry the King. One thing was very certain. The King was totally and utterly infatuated with Wallis.

One diarist wrote at the time:

'It appears that the King is Mrs Simpson's devoted slave, and will go nowhere she is not invited.'

The drama which was enacted over Mrs Simpson's divorce, the pressure from the newspapers, the flight from France hotly pursued by the Press, the stoning of the windows of her house in Cumberland Place, and the tragic Abdication of the King are all part of history.

No one in England could believe that the King would give up his Throne. Abroad in the Colonies it seemed even more incredible.

But the King was so in love, and was determined to marry Wallis, even if it meant giving up the Throne and an Empire covering a quarter of the earth's surface.

Neither of them, however, really believed it would happen. Wallis was heard to say:

'The rabble will never let you go!'

I saw the plans they made for Buckingham Palace, to take away a lot of the beautiful alterations made by George V.

The marriage took place in France of the Duke of Windsor and the Duchess with no Royal rank.

It was certainly not very impressive. It was greeted with great sadness by many of the people who had watched the Prince grow up. From a young boy who did not get on with his Father he became the 'smiling Prince Charming' who captivated everyone he met.

They wished him happiness in his retirement from everything to which he had been educated. It seemed impossible to think that he could live without it.

Perhaps Mrs. Baldwin, the Prime Minister's wife, summed it all up in one sentence:

'God grant him peace and happiness but never an understanding of what he has lost!'

When I was married in December 1936 to Hugh McCorquodale, we went to Paris for our honeymoon. We went to have luncheon at the famous Maxim's

Restaurant and there were the Prince of Wales and Wallis also on their honeymoon.

He had gone off to the 'Gentlemen's' and she was waiting for him.

I thought: 'Shall I curtsy or shall I not curtsy?'

I had previously asked Edwina Mountbatten what she was going to do in this situation, and she had said:

'Well, if it makes him happy, what does it matter? I curtsy to anyone if it makes them happy.'

So I gave Wallis a bob and she said to me:

'I hope you will be as happy as we are.'

My husband, who did not speak French, went into the 'Gentlemen's' and a man tried to stop him, saying: '*Non! Non, Monsieur!*'

But he paid no attention and walked on, and found the Prince of Wales there.

Of course he knew him, so they had a long talk, and when they came out I curtsied, and we all moved into the restaurant.

We were at a middle table, and they were on a sofa at the side with a lot of friends who were all talking and laughing when suddenly the Prince said:

'I want some butter! Butter, waiter! Butter!' all in English.

No one paid the slightest attention!

I thought how sad! He was once the most important King in the world, and now no one attends to him when he just wants a pat of butter.

The Abdication of King Edward VIII was a stunning blow which made it difficult for the Duke and Duchess of York to realise at first what it would mean to them.

It was in the woods of St Paul's Walden Bury, Hertfordshire, H.R.H. Prince Albert, Duke of York, second son of George V, begged Lady Elizabeth Bowes-Lyon to marry him. They had met at a dance three years earlier, and although the Duke was very shy and found it hard to express his feelings, he realised later he had fallen in love.

It was not surprising. As someone wrote: 'Her radiant vitality, and a blending of gaiety, kindness and sincerity made her irresistible to men.'

Lady Elizabeth Bowes-Lyon also had, beneath her soft, gentle manner, a good sense of humour and an enjoyment of the ridiculous.

When the Duke told his Father whom he wanted to marry, George V merely replied: 'You will be lucky if she accepts you.'

The Duke was unlucky and Lady Elizabeth did refuse him, but they continued to meet. Again she refused him, but there was still hope because the Duke was invited to Glamis, the great Castle of the Strathmore family in Scotland.

Afterwards Lady Strathmore wrote of her daughter:

'I think Elizabeth was torn between her longing to make Bertie happy and her reluctance to take on the big responsibilities which the marriage must bring.'

But in the New Year Bertie sent a telegram to his parents at Sandringham in the code they had arranged. It said simply, 'ALL RIGHT BERTIE.'

The Royal Family were delighted at the engagement.

The King, who never expressed his emotions or feelings very strongly, wrote to his son:

Dearest Bertie, you are indeed a lucky man to have such a charming and delightful wife as Elizabeth, and I am sure you will both be very happy together. I wish you both may have many, many years before you and you will be as happy as Mama and I are after you have been married for thirty years. I cannot wish you more.

Ever, my dear boy,

your most devoted Papa, G.R.

The King gave Elizabeth an ermine fur coat as a wedding present, but the young Duchess of York in 1926 was to give the Royal Family a gift beyond value.

There was a great rejoicing when their first daughter, who was named Elizabeth after her mother, was born.

The marriage was very happy and the Duchess of York was just the right person to help her husband get over a slight impediment in his speech.

The first time I saw the Duchess of York was when my daughter Raine presented her with a bouquet.

Raine was only a year and nine months at the time and the bouquet was almost as big as she was. But the Duchess, with her usual sweet charm, took it from her and charmed Raine at the same time.

The Duchess was, I thought, very pretty, but she did not have the outstanding beauty she was to acquire later.

She and the Duke continued to live a more or less quiet life together, occasionally going abroad, but not being very much in the public eye until the drama and, to the Royal family, the horror, of the Abdication occurred.

Earl Mountbatten later told me that when King Edward VIII decided to give up the throne, the Duke of York said to him:

'This cannot be happening to me! This is terrible, Dickie! I never wanted it to happen. I am quite unprepared for it. David has been trained all his life to be King, while I have never even seen a State Paper. I am a Naval Officer. It is the only thing I know about!'

After he had heard a servant call him 'Your Majesty' at Fort Belvedere before the ex-King left England, Prince Bertie returned to London to see his Mother.

Queen Mary had always been thought of as a very stiff, magnificent, but unsympathetic person.

Her son rested his head on her shoulder and wept.

When someone spoke to her of what had occurred, Queen Mary said:

'The person who needs most sympathy is my second son. He is the one who is making the sacrifice.'

There was no doubt there was a certain lack of confidence nationally in the Duke of York. They felt with his speech impediment he would not be a dramatic enough personality to be King.

They had, however, not realised that the strong, resilient Scottish blood in the Queen would enable her to turn the whole situation to the advantage of Great Britain.

When the War came, and I was the only Lady Welfare Officer for the Services in Bedfordshire, with 20,000 troops to look after, I was very lucky in that near me was the Queen's eldest brother, Major Michael Bowes-Lyon.

His wife became one of my greatest friends and we worked together on the enormous problems which existed amongst the Service personnel.

In the previous war, Fergus Bowes-Lyon was killed at Loos in 1915, and in 1917 his younger brother Michael was reported missing.

The Bowes-Lyons were broken-hearted when the War Office announced that he had been killed.

David, the third son was brought home from school to be with his parents.

There was only fifteen months in age between David and Elizabeth. They did everything together and were very close.

At luncheon one day one of the family pointed out to David that he should not wear coloured clothes and a coloured tie so soon after his brother Michael's death.

'Michael is not dead,' David protested. 'I have seen him twice. He is in a big house surrounded by fir-trees. He is not dead, but I think he is very ill because his head is tied up in a cloth.'

The family knew that David as a child had the uncanny Scottish gift of 'fey' which means 'second sight'.

Only Elizabeth believed him on this occasion.

The rest pointed out that the War Office had reported Michael killed, and they were not likely to have made a mistake.

David would not listen.

'Michael is not dead!' he maintained. 'I have seen him twice, and I am not wearing mourning for him!'

Three months later David was proved right. Michael had been shot through the head and it was some time before he recovered his mental powers.

He was therefore unable to let his family know that he was a prisoner in a prison hospital in Germany.

Michael, when I met him, was commanding the Home Guard at Biggleswade in Bedfordshire, as my husband was running it in Great Barford, where we lived.

Hugh had not been able to go to the Second World War because he had been so badly wounded in the First.

The Queen came down frequently to see her brother and also, needless to say, to help us with the troops in Bedfordshire.

I think few people at the time realised how hard the Royal Family worked during the War, because their activities were often 'hush-hush'.

I remember what the Queen did at Biggleswade seemed to me fantastic, but I was told it was not unduly hard.

It was a Sunday and she attended Divine Service before leaving London.

On the way to Bedfordshire she stopped to inspect some Boy Scouts, which of course meant meeting innumerable people.

She arrived at her brother's house in time for luncheon, then they drove to Biggleswade Cricket Ground where the Home Guard was on parade.

The Queen walked down the lines over the rough ground, stopping frequently to talk to the men. It took a long time.

I reckoned she must have travelled at least two

miles in her high-heeled pearl-grey shoes which she wore on her little feet. The size she takes is three and a half.

After taking the salute, the Queen went into a marquee where a great number of people were presented to her.

There were not only the Home Guard officers and their wives, but also the dignitaries of the County. She said a few words to nearly everyone and talked happily to those sitting near her at tea.

After that she drove back to her brother's house through cheering crowds, to inspect the Red Cross Detachment, speaking to every adult member of every Link.

Then she got into a car and drove off to Bedford to meet the American troops who had just arrived.

I took her round them, and I wish I could remember all the things the men said about her afterwards.

They simply adored the easy way she talked to them, and her simple, direct manner.

More than one man remarked wonderingly:

'I didn't know Queens were like that!'

Another man said:

'She talked to me about my bicycle. Now who'd have thought a Queen would know anything about cycling?'

It was nine-thirty before the Queen got home to dinner, a huge day, but quite a usual one in the service of the King's people.

One more incident. During dinner that evening she dropped a spot of gravy on her dress.

'This is my Show Gown!' she exclaimed.

We were all on coupons and clothes were precious. The Queen ran upstairs and changed!

I have always admired Queen Elizabeth, now the Queen Mother, more than any other woman. She has never put a foot wrong and she has the amazing capacity of making everyone she meets feel happy because she is there.

H.M. Queen Elizabeth the Queen Mother must, I am sure, have felt extremely proud when her beloved Grandson Charles was joined in matrimony to the Lady Diana Spencer.

When my daughter married the 8th Earl Spencer his youngest daughter Diana was only sixteen.

She found great enjoyment in reading my books and her Father took a photograph of her sitting up in bed with three Barbara Cartland novels with her.

She was very quiet, sweet and gentle. When Diana was seventeen I said to my daughter that I thought it was extraordinary that she was so kind to my youngest Grandson Henry who was then only eleven.

She took him to the cinema; they used to swim together and she was always trying to amuse him in one way or another.

It was later when she became famous throughout the world for her love for children that I realised it was psychological because she came from a broken home.

She had only been five when her Mother left her and her brother Charles was only three.

However the whole world went wild at the thought of the Prince of Wales, who Dickie

Mountbatten had said would one day make a great King, being married.

They thought he must have a sweet, gentle virgin just like the heroines in my books. No one fitted into the picture better than Diana Spencer.

In fact there was so much excitement about it that I said to my son-in-law, Lord Spencer:

'It is the first time in history a future Queen of England has ever been chosen by referendum.'

There has been so much written about the Wedding that it is very difficult now for people to realise the excitement and thrill of it all.

Since then, one commotion after another has filled the newspapers some of which is true but a great deal of which is untrue.

Lord Mountbatten's Secretary, who died recently, had written, to get money, a most appalling book which was the last thing one had ever expected of him.

He had always been, I thought, devoted to Lord Mountbatten and we were all very fond of him. However, after the tragedy of Lord Mountbatten's death he became a changed person.

In his book he said very unkind and untrue things about Lord Mountbatten which should never have been published.

He was also incredibly rude about Prince Michael and Princess Marie-Christine. They had been so kind to him by not only financing him after Lord Mountbatten's death, but had offered him a position in their household.

Where I was concerned he wrote, for no reason I could ascertain, a lie saying I had asked him almost on my knees to find me a place in St. Paul's Cathedral for the Royal Wedding.

The truth of the matter is something quite simple and there was no reason for him to lie in such an extraordinary manner.

My son-in-law, because he was the father of the bride, expected to have at least five hundred seats to give to his family, his close friends and those who worked with him on the enormous number of charity organisations he patronised.

But as so many people wished to come from abroad to attend the Wedding – apart from the huge demand at home – St. Paul's Cathedral was actually not big enough for the number of people who wished to see the two young people united in Holy Matrimony. My son-in-law therefore received only fifty seats and he very kindly sent me two. One for myself and one for Ian.

I thought that it was an occasion which the young people would want to remember in the years to come. Therefore it would be far wiser for my two sons to attend it together.

Actually as I was nearly eighty I was rather nervous about having to spend such a long time sitting in the cathedral as was inevitable.

I was quite right.

Ian and Glen left Whitehall Court at nine o'clock in the morning.

At the very last moment someone was ill or died and Raine sent them an extra ticket for Ian's wife, Anna.

They arrived at St. Paul's and eventually left at two o'clock which I would have found an intolerable time at my age.

Instead I asked the St. John people who had been on the procession route all night to come to Camfield on their way back to have something to eat and drink.

For those who got here early we watched the Wedding taking place on the television. I wore, for the last time, my St. John uniform.

It was after the Royal Wedding, at the request of one of the newspapers that I wrote a book called *Romantic Royal Marriages*, commencing with William the Conqueror, travelling through the ages and ending with Their Royal Highnesses, Prince Charles and Princess Diana.

Underneath were the words: '... and they lived happily ever after.' It was wishful thinking but very sincerely meant at the time.

I am extremely concerned at the prospect that in the future we might lose our Royal Family.

'Land of hope and glory ...' Can we really sing that convincingly today?

Our Royal Family has been and still is the envy of the world. But it is being criticised and questioned in a manner which has never happened before.

It is often quoted that a country in decline turns inward on itself and starts to question the institutions that have made that country great.

I would never accept that Great Britain is a country in decline but there is no doubt that we are not as great and powerful as we were fifty, a hundred, or a hundred and fifty years ago.

At the moment many of our institutions of State are under attack from all directions. Our political system, the Church, the Law, the Armed Forces and above all the Constitution itself and even more importantly the role of the Monarchy.

I believe that we as a Nation must stop this debilitating rush towards self-destruction.

When we read the newspapers today and listen to the News on the television and radio, it is like a doom-laden liturgy of the Nation's ills.

The pound devalued and still falling, new job losses at the heart of our manufacturing industries, another horror story of children in care, and a scandal suggested about a prominent figure in public life.

No wonder people are feeling depressed and dispirited about our current situation.

Ronald Reagan, when he was President of the United States, was a man of great determination and guts.

He lifted his country out of the malaise of Watergate, the Iranian hostages and the economic stagnation by telling the Americans how great and good they were.

He invested them with confidence and pride in their country and abilities, to the extent that they believed it all and it became a reality.

We can do it too and lift ourselves out of the gloom and doom all around us.

We have so much to be proud of, so much that is envied by other countries, and we have a brilliant future in an uncertain world if only we can reverse our national inferiority complex and start planning positively for our future, and that of our children and grandchildren.

Throughout our history we have looked to our

great leaders for hope and inspiration. One can think of Marlborough, Wellington, Disraeli and Churchill who contributed so much to our greatness.

But we look to the Head of State, the Monarch, as the ultimate power and authority over us all. The Monarchy that goes on and continues, that survives Politics, Politicians and Policies, that is the rock on which our country rests and to whom we all turn in times of trouble and danger.

What is happening to our Monarchy today? The Royal Family is under such attack for the conduct of their personal lives that it is calling into question the position, role and authority of the Monarchy itself.

It is trivia, tilting at the awesome power of the State. It is the tabloid Press that makes the news headlines with the sensationalism of every little piece of tittle-tattle and gossip.

What does this lead to? It leads to the diminution of us all, our ideals, our hopes and beliefs in all our cherished certainties of life in Britain in the 1990s.

The Queen had a bad year in 1992. Her family let her down. She needs to consolidate her position and to restore the nation's confidence in the Monarchy after all the knocks, the scandal and the innuendo.

What many people do not realize is that for the British there is no reasonable alternative to our Monarchy, its position as the Head of State and the embodiment of our Constitution.

The Queen's patronage is enormous. Everything imaginable is done in the name of the Queen, from Her Majesty's Prisons to the Royal Mail, from Her Majesty's Stationery Office to the Royal County of Berkshire, from The Queen's Speech at the Opening of Parliament, to the Royal Assent to every Act of Parliament on which is based our Royal Legal System.

To replace all this with a republic or a diminished Royal role is unthinkable. It would only add to our decline and to our continuing inferiority complex.

Almost every other country in Europe is thinking of having Royalty again including the French, the Italians and the Germans.

The countries that were behind the Iron Curtain, Hungary, Czechoslovakia and Poland are also considering it. They realize, if we do not, that Royalty means continuity and stability.

If we lose Buckingham Palace, the Changing of the Guard and the Aristocratic houses which are open to the public, we will certainly lose our tourists which would be a tremendous loss and expense to everyone.

Despite the Recession sixteen million people visited England in 1991.

We must now rally to our Flag, our Country and above all to our belief in ourselves.

Prince Charles, if he was allowed to use it has – as Lord Mountbatten said so often – the most brilliant brain any English King has had for centuries. With the help of God and our Prayers, England will be great again and lead the world as we have in the past.

# Chapter Five

So much has been written about Lord Mountbatten that it is not difficult for people to realise how different he was in so many ways from the rather complacent men of his age.

One thing I think few people realise is that it was he who introduced the idea of Royalty shaking hands on every important occasion. In fact he introduced it to the Royal Family.

It started when he took over his first ship and asked his officers to find out everything they could which was personal about his crew.

Because he had the most amazing memory which I have always called a 'Royal' memory, he learnt from the list something about every man serving with him.

Then when he took over the ship he had them all on deck and he went round shaking hands, which no other Captain had ever done, with every man who was to serve with him.

Because he had learnt about them he would say:

'How-do-you-do, Watson?' (Or whatever his name was.) 'I do hope your Mother is better.'

He passed on to the next man to say:

'I expect your twins will miss you while you are away.'

The crew was absolutely astonished.

It was something which had never happened to them before.

It was then Lord Mountbatten said to his wife Edwina, who was my greatest friend, and to me:

'You must always shake hands with anyone to whom you are speaking.'

Edwina I had known since her father and mine became great friends at the time of the General Election in 1910 when we were both nine years old.

She became so enthusiastic about the St. John Ambulance Brigade that she would shake hands with everyone on Parade which often took a very long time.

When I was speaking, especially about 'health', I always went down into the audience afterwards, if I could, and shook hands with everyone present.

It was therefore entirely Lord Mountbatten's idea which has now been taken up by the Royal Family.

For the first time a Queen has shaken hands with a crowd applauding her.

There were so many things one might say about Lord Mountbatten.

But perhaps it was his charm and real interest in the people with whom he associated which made him so popular and loved everywhere he went.

He also had the vibrations of personality which is so lacking in many of our politicians today. He had that 'Star Quality' which made him noticeable the moment he walked into a room. He also had the enthusiasm and power of leadership which is something that at the moment we sadly miss both politically and individually.

One story which he used to tell and which I think reveals the amazing effect he had on people was of when he visited the soldiers who had been in Burma, whom one seldom heard about. In fact Lord Mountbatten was quite convinced they had been forgotten.

When he appeared amongst them he stood on the nearest box, which was something he always advised me to do, so that he could be seen by all those present.

'Men!' he shouted in a deep voice which still carried surprisingly well. 'Men! You probably think that Burma is the forgotten front. You're wrong! It's never been heard of!'

There was a pause and then he went on:

'But it is going to be and you are going to be. You are going to be known all over the world for what you are going to do.'

When he finished there was a tremendous applause and he knew that he had lifted the men out of their gloom and despondency into something very different.

Since my husband had died I had been desperately unhappy and lonely without him. Dickie Mountbatten had also been very lonely after Edwina had died in 1960.

We had therefore seen a great deal of each other. One of the marvellous things was that we had known each other for so long and our families had been so united, Edwina and her sister Mary being my greatest friends, that we had a background of mutual friends and mutual experiences which was very comforting. I stayed whenever I wanted to at his house at Broadlands.

Dickie Mountbatten had always wanted to do what other people were doing, so he said to me one day:

'I think you make more money out of your novels than any other kind of book. Therefore I want a novel from you for the United World Colleges.'

This was a subject very close to his heart because he believed that when the students from different countries in the world worked together at the college, they would eventually grow to understand one another and there would be no more wars.

I said I would be delighted to do a book but that he must help me.

He was only too eager to do so.

I said that he was to do the plot for *Love at the Helm* then I would do the love. In my story there was a very attractive passenger on board who fell in love with the handsome captain.

Dickie and I had written five chapters when he was assassinated. I therefore had to finish it without him.

When it was finished and published it received a great deal of attention because he was part of it.

I think one of the great experiences I had at Broadlands was to see Dickie and Douglas Fairbanks together. They were undoubtedly the two most handsome and interesting men in the world.

Both were very tall, very vivacious with the extraordinary star quality, which I have already described Dickie had. They were fascinating when they were together.

I do not know whether people in this country realise how much Douglas did for our country during the

War; he has twelve Honours and Awards, including Knight Commander of the Most Excellent Order of the British Empire and Knight of Justice of the Most Venerable Order of the Hospital of St. John of Jerusalem, these being just two from this country, together with the Distinguished Service Cross.

In 1984 I went out to Florida to speak at their Round Table Intellectual Forum. Douglas was to introduce me and I was to be the Speaker.

We were both rather gratified to find that they had sold out completely and they had never had such a large number of people asking for tickets, as they had had for us.

Douglas was in tremendous form, very amusing and afterwards Bea Cayzer, the American who married one of our great racehorse owners, gave a special party for us in their house which is in the centre of Palm Beach.

The wine flowed and the one person who certainly missed none of it was Lord Carnarvon, whom I had known for many, many years, and who had grown rather old and unsteady in the last months of his life.

The party was typically American because everybody enjoyed themselves so much. The Americans, far more than us, seem to understand how to laugh all the time and to really enjoy meeting their friends.

Douglas Fairbanks gave a party for us in his delightful house, which has a water garden, and we found it difficult to tear ourselves away when finally we had to go home.

At Douglas's party, I sat next to a man who was very attractive and who flirted with me so easily, which the Americans are exceptionally good at.

He then told me that the one thing in which he believed for his health, was Super Oxide Dismutase (S.O.D.) which made him feel so young and virile. It is said to slow down the ageing process and to give a longer and healthier life.

I said to him:

'Well you are very enthusiastic about it, but you are really too young yet to be a judge as to whether it will last when you grow older.'

He said:

'How old do you think I am?'

I replied that I thought he was about thirty-two or thirty-three.

He laughed and said:

'I am actually sixty-three!'

I was absolutely astounded. But at the same time I knew that he was quite right in saying that S.O.D. was an exceptional product, I believe in it myself and know that Douglas does, too.

I shall always think of Florida as a place of laughter with people who go out of their way to be friendly and charming to everyone they meet.

But to return to Lord Mountbatten, in August 1979 Dickie was going out to Ireland where he spent a certain amount of time at his castle. His family went with him and also several friends and relations.

I said goodbye to him at the beginning of the week, he was leaving at the weekend. On Thursday his Secretary telephoned to say he wanted to see me.

I have thought since that he had a sudden premonition that something might happen.

As I said to his Secretary:

'Why does he want to see me?'

To which he replied:

'I don't know. His Lordship just said he wants to see you.'

So I went to London although it was very hot and I had other plans. I found that he had nothing particular to say but, as he said, he just wanted to see me.

We had a very enjoyable luncheon. Then when I was going back to the country I said:

'I hate you going to Ireland.'

'Do not worry,' he said, 'I have nineteen guards to look after me.'

'Nineteen!' I exclaimed. 'But I signed books for thirty-six last year.'

'Oh yes,' he replied, 'but the Prime Minister said as I am so popular in the village they will let me know if anything is happening.'

This meant that sitting comfortably in his castle the guard did not look at his boat.

I was having luncheon with my son Glen when the butler came in and said he had just heard on the radio that Earl Mountbatten had been assassinated.

It was a terrible shock but it was no use then saying we should have taken further precautions.

Dickie had arranged his funeral so beautifully that the man who was in charge of it only came to London the very day it was taking place.

Sometimes when we were going out to dinner he would say:

'I have been choosing the hymns to be played at my funeral.'

I used to reply:

'Shut up! I cannot bear you to talk like that.'

But he said he would hate it to be badly organised.

He was a marvellous organiser and needless to say his funeral service was superb.

The Prince of Wales took part in it. Dickie had always referred to Charles as the son he had never had.

It was fortunate that he had spent almost the last month of his life with Prince Charles who was working at Portsmouth and had therefore slept at Broadlands.

It was a very moving service and the arrangements were excellent. They had organised a cinema screen on the columns so one could see the procession coming towards the church.

The Queen said afterwards that what had upset her and what certainly upset me was when we saw his favourite charger with the Earl's riding boots turned backwards which is the form when someone is dead.

I received an invitation (overleaf) to attend the ceremony for the unveiling of the Memorial Statue of the Earl Mountbatten.

I feel sure Dickie would have loved every moment of the pomp and circumstances of the occasion.

There were massed Bands, Anthems, Flags and nineteen members of the Royal Family. Thirteen foreign Crowned heads and their families travelled to our shores, five Prime Ministers were present, and a large slice of our British Aristocracy.

We all sat in solemn mood, to watch Her Majesty the Queen unveil Lord Mountbatten's statue.

In the fine rain it was a very moving moment when three women – a reigning Monarch, a daughter who was still grieving for her father, and a powerful

The Prime Minister and Her Majesty's Government
request the honour of the company of

*Miss Barbara Cartland*

at the Unveiling of the Memorial Statue of
Admiral of The Fleet The Earl Mountbatten of Burma
KG, PC, GCB, OM, GCSI, GCIE, GCVO, DSO
by
Her Majesty The Queen
on The Foreign Office Green, Horse Guards Parade
at 11 am on Wednesday 2nd November 1983
followed by a Reception at The Banqueting House, Whitehall

*If you accept this invitation the appropriate
tickets and instructions will be sent to you*

*You will be asked to be seated by 10.25 am*

RSVP on the enclosed card
by 23 September 1983
Ministry of Defence PS 12 (Army)
Room 337 Lansdowne House
Berkeley Square LONDON W1X 6AA

THIS CARD WILL NOT ADMIT

woman – climbed the steps to the base of the monu-
ment standing eighteen feet.

The Queen, Countess Mountbatten and Mrs. Thatcher bowed their heads for a few seconds, each in
their own memories of him – then the Queen pulled
the small cord and the huge Union Jack covering the
statue fell silently to the ground.

We all saw him in gleaming bronze, in his naval
'day' uniform, with one hand clenched behind his
back, a pair of binoculars gripped in the other.

He looks out across the green outside the Foreign
Office, on Horse Guards Parade, and stares at his old
office The Admiralty building.

The Queen looked wonderful in her peacock-blue

Margaret Wigham, Duchess of Argyll *(top left)*, was the most beautiful débutante of her year; the Marquis of Bath *(top right)* had an interesting and romantic double wedding; Lord Brocket *(bottom left)* has one of the most delightful houses in England; The Duke of Sutherland *(bottom right)*, the most handsome Duke I have ever known.

Lord Mountbatten persuaded me to write a novel with him which could be sold for the United World Colleges, a cause very close to his heart.

In this picture I found myself between the two most intelligent, handsome and delightful men I have ever known, Lord Mountbatten and Sir Arthur Bryant.

Douglas Fairbanks Junior with Lord Mountbatten.

The most intelligent woman I have ever known, whom I admire more than anyone else, is the Queen Mother. Here she is looking radiant on her wedding day.

The Queen Mother inspecting the Home Guard – who adored her as everyone else in the country adored her during the war. She not only comforted and helped this country to victory but inspired everyone with whom she came into contact.

This photograph, taken by my son-in-law, shows his daughter Diana reading one of my books, which she always enjoyed.

This picture of Princess Diana *(left)* was from my book *Romantic Royal Marriages*, which was published at the time of her wedding to Prince Charles. Prince Charles in uniform *(right)*. Lord Mountbatten always said he would make a great King.

I was the first person to have a white Rolls-Royce in England. It was one of the first white cars on the road. People stared in astonishment and asked if they could photograph it.

My Magic Tree, planted by Princess Elizabeth, later Queen Elizabeth I, in 1550 when she was more or less a prisoner at Hatfield House.

My first Pekingese was named Twi-
Twi because I had just been to
Taiwan when he was born.

This horse, named Amber Lance,
was given to me to run in the name
of the St. John Ambulance Brigade.

In one of the rooms at Camfield Place which I call the Royal Bedroom.

coat and cowboy-style hat, which was a very stark contrast to Mrs. Thatcher's elegant black ensemble.

The Queen's address to all those present came through as a celebration of the life of Lord Mountbatten and the whole Royal Family were joined in these sentiments.

Someone who created a certain joyfulness was Prince Edward who arrived wearing his Royal Marine Officer's overcoat, which seemed several sizes too large for him, and with a huge cap on his head.

Princess Anne was the first member of the Family to joke about his enormous outfit, and Prince Andrew dug his brother in the ribs rather playfully.

Unfortunately we could not see the reaction on Prince Edward's face because of his enormous cap.

One thing I found out during the passing years is that no one has ever forgotten Lord Mountbatten and only very recently I had luncheon with the Duke of Abercorn and we talked for a long time about Dickie. How we both loved him and how we could never forget what he meant to the world and to us.

I miss Dickie more than I can possibly say. We had known each other over fifty years. I went up to London once or twice a week to have luncheon or dinner with him.

He was the most marvellous person in that he inspired conversation, and it was impossible not to enjoy every moment of being with him.

He too enjoyed talking and listening. One night when I was staying at Broadlands we talked until two o'clock in the morning. He said it was one of the best evenings we had ever had.

Everybody who knew him knew that he had this magical way of making ordinary conversation seem brilliant and witty. One was only sorry it had to end.

I thought it would have pleased him if I had asked the 'Lower Deck', which he always loved so sincerely, to write their reminiscences which could be published.

We would also have just a few of his close friends to write about him and give their recollections.

One of these was Prince Rainier of Monaco, who wrote to me saying that he considered Lord Mountbatten to be a 'real man', with all the human and moral values and the qualities of heart and spirit with a constant search for humour. He spoke of him as having the roughness of a sailor and the authority of a Leader.

He concluded by stating that he had great charm, was ready to help all, everything that happened in the world interested him, his knowledge was vast, and his humour was lively.

I had collected not only a great number of letters but also excellent photographs, but the publishers said that there had been too much on Lord Mountbatten and I could not get anyone to publish them.

H.R.H. Prince Michael of Kent was very sorry that the publishers would not take the Mountbatten book and he felt sure that they would do so in the future.

Earl Mountbatten was Viceroy of India for a number of years and always held India close to his heart as I do.

When I first visited India in 1959, I stayed with the Governor of Bombay. He said:

'Oh do speak to my women and tell them about

your vitamins, I am sure they will be interested.'

I spoke to a large number of women who had no idea what I was talking about. I then realised that India, at that time, was not interested in vitamins.

Later, when Indira Gandhi became Prime Minister and I sent her vitamins every year, she distributed them to her staff who wrote me lovely letters saying how much good they were doing.

Then, unexpectedly, a marvellous person called Princess Shahnaz started to introduce to India their own vitamins from the Himalayas.

They were such a success that, due entirely to her, they erected a large Health Resort thirteen miles from Delhi on a hundred acres of land and asked me to open it.

It is exactly what I wanted people to have. It is called 'Body and Soul' and not only has all my vitamins and everything else I recommended, but also has a place for meditation and yoga.

I went to India in 1988 with Ian and arrived in Delhi on March 13th. The weather was lovely and I was able to wear a large pink hat and a thin dress.

When I arrived at the Health Resort, there was a huge reception of girls who greeted me enthusiastically. They threw rose-buds on the path on which I had to walk to perform the opening.

They gave me a cake decorated with rose-buds which said on it 'We love you Barbara.'

There were rose petals to greet me when I entered the building. I then cut the ribbon to launch the opening of the Health Resort.

In my opening speech I said:

'India has got a unique place in the community of

nations because of its spiritual and moral power.'

'Moral standards,' I said, 'all over Europe and America have gone down to such an extent that it's terrifying even to think about them.'

Later that evening I shook hands with a great number of women and received a present of a very delightful plate from the Government.

I also received a letter from Rajiv, the Prime Minister, whom I had known since he was a little boy, saying as he was electioneering he was so sorry he could not be with me, but the next time I came he would give me a special party.

I never dreamt that before I would go to India again he would be assassinated.

I have always been only too eager to travel around the world to publicise my 'health' crusade.

Maurice Hanssen who runs the official side of the Health Food Traders took me to Austria in 1969 at the invitation of the Mayor of Vienna, for a special dinner party given for me because of my contribution to Health.

We had a delicious dinner in the Mayor's Parlour and afterwards danced on the carpet to the tune of 'The Blue Danube'.

Many years later, in 1986, I was asked to go to Vienna again and I stayed, with Ian, at the famous Sacher Hotel. It is one of the oldest hotels in Europe and just as attractive as I expected it to be.

Our suite was all in white and the food exactly what one might expect. I was taken down to the kitchen and saw them making the famous Sacher cake which is delicious. The recipe was left as a legacy by the famous chef Edward Sacher.

Everyone who goes to Vienna wants a taste of it regardless of what it does to the figure!

When I arrived I said there were two things I really wanted to do.

I wanted to sing on the biggest stage in the world which was where Wagner played a lot of his music.

Secondly, I wanted to be photographed at the famous Spanish Riding School with the white stallions, where the Empress of Austria had ridden.

They said both things were impossible but I was able to do both eventually because I was being filmed.

I went to the Royal Opera House in the afternoon in full evening-dress, went onto the main stage and was filmed miming to my own singing of 'Mr. Wonderful', which I had sung with the Royal Philharmonic Orchestra.

I did not think there would be an audience but there were a lot of English visitors who thought it was a show put on for them and they applauded loudly.

Years ago when I was writing biographies, I wrote a biography of Elizabeth Empress of Austria.

It was taken by the Elizabeth Club who said it was the best biography ever written about her. They told Lord Mountbatten how pleased they were with it when he visited Vienna.

She has always been one of my favourite Royal personages and I loved writing the book. Every memory of her was more attractive than the last, including of course when she came to England and Ireland to hunt because we had such good horses.

When Ian and I left Vienna we travelled to Munich and stayed in a very comfortable hotel. We realised that people were coming to the Summer Beer Festival from all over the country.

We could see it best from the top of the hotel where there was a swimming pool.

We watched the people processing below us. What worried me slightly was that all the horses and carts coming from the country had their attendants walking with them and someone could easily have been hurt. They marched better than any trained soldiers could do as they passed through the cheering crowds.

We watched the famous Games and I was taken round by the *Bürgermeister*.

I returned to Munich eight years later, and appeared in a late-night talk show which is the most popular one on German television.

I asked them how long I should be on and they said:

'Under ten minutes,' which of course is quite usual even though it is a long way to go for such a short appearance.

However, I was beautifully arranged on a sofa which showed off my dress and was given an earpiece to put in my ear. The same thing had happened in France in 1991, and I, rather stupidly, thought that, as in France, what I said would be translated. Instead of which what the interviewer said was translated into English for me.

As it was translated by a woman who spoke in a very guttural voice I did not understand one word.

However I realised there was nothing I could do once the curtain had gone up and a man started to interview me.

Then to my surprise I realised there was a large audience in the Studio. As I could not understand a word he said to me I just talked.

To my astonishment I was allowed to go on for twenty-nine and a half minutes! They said I was brilliant although I did not answer the questions, which was not surprising considering I did not understand them.

During my travels I very often experience the most amusing moments.

In October 1980 I was asked if I would design for one of the biggest companies in America and give them some ideas for their curtains, furnishings and wall coverings.

I arrived in New York in 1981 with Ian and my hairdresser, Mrs. Austen, whom I had asked particularly to come with me, as she had been with me for more than thirty years.

When I had visited America before I had had a dresser whom I found not very effective. She spent most of the time counting the flowers I had received which would be hers when I left.

So I insisted this time that they paid for my hairdresser to come with me. She was a great success in the way she looked after me and everyone found her absolutely charming.

She was, however, amused when we arrived and was told:

'If you want to go out with a man in New York, you have to go out with the taxi drivers because they are the real men as they are mostly Greek, Swiss, French or English.'

It seemed American men at that time in New York were very busy with each other.

My hairdresser replied coolly: 'I do not often go out with taxi drivers.'

However, we enjoyed our trip immensely except that they were having trouble in Ireland and I was told that, as I was the nearest thing at that moment to Royalty, I was in danger.

I was therefore given two Secret Service men to protect me.

They walked each side of me whenever I left the hotel. On one occasion when I had just been on television at the Rockefeller Building, as we walked towards the road, one man ran ahead to see if the car was there.

He came back and said in a hissing voice:

'Look out on the right!'

Then they walked in front of me with their hands stuffed into their coat pockets. As we reached the road there was a poor old man leaning against a wall. He put his hand into his breast pocket and the two Security men pulled out their revolvers and pointed them at him.

What the old man had in his hand when he pulled it from his pocket was a pencil and he said to me:

'Please may I have your autograph.'

After that excitement in New York we went on to Denver.

We stayed in a most extraordinary hotel which had once been a prison. The rooms all seemed very small and opened on to the centre of the building.

We then drove to Colorado Springs with a very smart man who told me that he collected Rolls-Royces and he had fifty-three.

When we arrived I was greeted with great enthusiasm, and everyone was dressed in pink for a ceremony at which I was given an Award which reads:

> To Barbara Cartland
> 1981 Woman of Achievement
> for Decorating with Love.
> National Home Fashions League

Some of the clothes worn by the people there were very strange and were obviously what they wore for swimming. Others had elaborate Ballgowns to which they attached roses and other flowers.

Nevertheless it was a compliment to me that they liked pink.

We had a lovely time and then we drove back to Denver. When I was taken to the airport the next day our chauffeur arrived with five Rolls-Royces all decorated with pink flowers. It was a very smart procession in which to leave.

I will always look back with deep affection at the kindness and enthusiasm of those Americans, which raises one's spirits far better than any champagne has ever done.

Way back in 1970 in America, I was selling a million copies of every book. At last the publishers had woken up to say to other writers: 'Write like Barbara Cartland, with pornography.'

The new authors of romantic novels remained very

loyal to me, and I returned to America to meet them in 1983.

The first thing they did was to organise a train which picked up writers from all across America and brought them to New York.

I met them at the station and they came out of the train singing to the tune of 'Hello, Dolly' – 'Hello, Barbara. Well, hello, Barbara. We're glad to have you back where you belong!'

They each carried a pink tulip.

The writers were attending a three-day Convention on romantic fiction and had signed autographs for fans all the way from California.

Limousines and horse-drawn buggies with pink balloons attached carried the writers to the Roosevelt Hotel.

I was asked the inevitable question: 'How do you catch a man?'

To which I replied:

'Use your intelligence and your imagination. Do not show him that you are as clever as he is, but that you are clever enough to let him think that he is cleverer than you.'

The Conference was to feature Awards for the best in romantic fiction and there were many speeches and workshops.

It was all wonderfully organised by Kathryn Falk, who is the author of *How to Write a Romance Novel and Get it Published*.

It was a fantastic show all together and entirely due to Kathryn who I think has proved herself the most marvellous organiser there has ever been. Anything more difficult than organising all those women

I cannot imagine! Her magazine is becoming more and more in demand every month.

Something extraordinary happened to me when I was visiting America in 1979.

I was promoting my Helena Rubenstein scent, and it was just before Christmas.

Helena Rubenstein had sent to me the whole range in beautiful boxes and put them under the Christmas tree in the large room where the reception was to be held, for me to give away to people as presents.

I stood at the door of the reception room waiting to receive people, when in came three men, dressed like porters from the hotel, and each was pushing a trolley.

They loaded their trollies with the presents from beneath the Christmas tree and I thought they were transferring them to where people could receive them when they left.

What I did not know until we came to look for the presents to give away, was that the men were stealing them, and had vanished. I have never, in my life, come across such a blatant form of theft.

At the reception I was asked many times the same question.

Is there love at first sight?

The answer is definitely 'Yes!' People have believed in 'Love at First Sight' since the beginning of time.

My Father went into a ballroom when he was twenty-three, saw my Mother dancing, and said: 'That is the girl I am going to marry!'

It took him a little time, but he married her. They

were blissfully happy until he was killed in World War I.

I have always believed that the Ancient Greeks were right when they said that when God first made Man he made a single being.

But the Man was lonely, so he was cut in half. The soft, sweet, gentle, spiritual side became the Woman; the fighting, authoritative and powerful half became the Man. Therefore, we go through life looking for the other half of ourselves.

Three-quarters of the world believes in the Wheel of Rebirth: if you fail to find your other half in this world, you have the chance of finding him or her in the world which comes later.

I fell in love at first sight once many years ago, in the South of France in Maxine Elliott's marvellous villa which still stands there.

I was introduced to a handsome young man, with whom I was told to play backgammon.

When we looked into each other's eyes it was impossible to move, impossible to think, except that he was exceptional in a way I could not put into words.

Unfortunately that had an unhappy ending but I have written a novel which is called *Love At First Sight* and I sincerely believe in it.

It is not only what you see in each other's eyes, but it is the vibrations which reach out towards each other. One knows instinctively that it is someone one has known before and who is part of oneself.

That is exactly what real love is. It is the love which comes from the heart and the soul. It is an instinct which seeps through the whole body, but it is in its effect a spiritual and emotional ecstasy.

It is what every woman hopes to find, and every man believes that one day will be his.

Of course there are disappointments, but in the thirty thousand letters I receive every year, a great number tell me they have found the ideal person, and are experiencing the real love about which I write. This is the love which comes from God and is part of God.

There is no argument against this for the simple reason it was given to us for the creation of a child and that in itself must make it Holy. It has nothing to do with the vulgarity and distortion of sex which is handed out to us every day by the media. Which is, in my opinion, doing a great deal of harm.

I have a great friend in America by the name of Richard Kirkam, who has helped me enormously over the years.

He became great friends with Father John Mericantante, who was the representative of the Vatican in the U.S.A.

He gave Father John the biography I had written of my Mother which impressed him very much.

As my Mother had become a Catholic in her old age, Richard and Father John went to Rome together and told the Pope about my Mother's biography and how she had been the head of 'The Sword and The Spirit' for six counties.

The Pope was very interested and said:

'I must send Barbara Cartland a present.'

He then blessed a rosary and sent it to me. He also promised to read the book when he had time as he reads English very well.

I thanked him profusely for the rosary which I keep by my bed and usually travel with when I am going on a long journey for protection.

I also take with me a bracelet with a cross on it which has been blessed and which has travelled already with me hundreds of thousands of miles.

What touched me very much was that when I had my ninetieth birthday the Pope remembered it and sent me another rosary which I also treasure.

For my ninetieth birthday I decided to have a party at Camfield.

It was lovely on the terrace looking down on to the lake and the wood beyond it. Everybody was entranced when they arrived at how beautiful it looked with all the tables set out prettily, and the coloured umbrellas, although the wind was ruffling them a little.

I had a huge pink cake with '90' on the top of it, which my chef Nigel had made, and with the pianist playing all the time it was, I thought, extremely romantic.

I noticed that in the party brought by Princess Helena Moutafian, who comes originally from Russia, there was a very good-looking elderly man with a very young girl beside him. I thought to myself:

'I wonder why he has brought his grandchild.'

He turned out to be the Member of Parliament Sir Anthony Buck, who was to be very much in the news because he was married to the beautiful Benvenida.

She, of course, hit the headlines when she was definitely not thinking or behaving like a grand-daughter even if she was looking like one!

One of the most unusual presents I had for my ninetieth birthday was a flamingo! In fact my Health people had actually sponsored a beautiful 'Pink Flamingo' at Whipsnade Zoo for the year in my name.

What I do find difficult when one gives a Garden Party is that one asks one's own friends, but, because it is in the garden, they think they can bring extra people.

One person arrived, whom I can still not connect in my mind, and who I was quite certain had not received an invitation, saying:

'I do hope that you do not mind, but I have brought my son, his friend and their friends with me.'

Well, I could not tell them to go away again, but I did think that it was rather a cheek. I had one person I did not think I had asked, and three people I had never met before!

I have come to the conclusion that it is more difficult for them to step through the door, when one is giving a party, than if they creep over the fence and come into the garden, betting they will not be turned away.

Also for my ninetieth birthday I had the most wonderful collection of flowers. The French particularly sent me enormous arrangements of carnations, including one which contained ninety pink carnations from one French publisher.

The whole house was full of glorious blossoms, from exotic arrangements to a wonderful bunch of sweet peas brought by a fan of mine from her garden locally.

We had a garden party on my birthday on a previous year in which we all had to squash into the barn because it suddenly started to pour with rain.

Fortunately the barn is very large and empty and everyone enjoyed themselves very much because I have always been quite certain that they like being herded together.

At my ninety-second birthday, however, disaster struck.

They had arranged, because it was my fiftieth year with St. John, that on my birthday they would plant an oak tree in my garden, with everybody local coming to see it.

Of course every St. John company in the county was represented. The children were terribly sweet in their uniforms, and they handed me a special spade decorated with pink ribbon with which to perform the ceremony.

The tree was to be planted on the raised ground outside the front door. We were all just about to proceed towards it when down came the rain in buckets full.

I therefore just had to look at the tree in the distance, and was photographed standing with the children and the President of St. John, Richard Walduck, at the front door. Fortunately it made such a good photograph that I thought I would have it for my Christmas card.

I was, however, somewhat disconcerted when I asked the newspaper, who took the photograph, if I could use it for my Christmas card, and they said they wanted £91.

I then got the President, Mr. Walduck, to write to them to say it would be a tremendous advantage to the St. John in Hertfordshire, if it could be used, and they most generously let me have it for nothing. It was, I think, one of the most successful Christmas cards I have ever had – I send out over a thousand cards each year, and all through the years we have tried to find different and amusing ones to go all over the world.

One of the guests I most enjoy entertaining on the occasion of my birthday celebrations is the tall, and extremely handsome, Lord Brocket.

He owns a lovely house in Hertfordshire with a very intriguing history. It is called Brocket Hall. It was the house where Melbourne died and, incidentally, as his servants stole from him he was much poorer than he should have been.

The garden was where Lady Caroline Lamb burnt love letters she had received from Lord Byron and danced round them while they were burning.

Lord Brocket married a very beautiful girl and I lent them my white Rolls and my chauffeur for the wedding, as he was having difficulty in those days running his house.

His Grandfather who was a very strange person and who was under house arrest during World War I, left all his money to his second son while his eldest son naturally inherited the title and this large and very beautiful house with wonderful ceilings and a large lake in front of it.

Since then Lord Brocket has been brilliant in making it one of the most important conference houses in the whole of England.

He gave me a special party there because I had helped him in many ways. I discovered he has to employ seventy-two servants to cope with the enormous number of people who stay there during the conferences.

A person who shares Lord Brocket's passion for cars is H.R.H. Prince Michael of Kent.

In November 1990 I was invited to Brooklands where many years earlier I had arranged the first motor race ever run with women drivers.

Prince Michael had been very keen to do something for Brooklands because he felt it was falling into disrepair and it was very important to the country.

It is still a very beautiful place and what we really wanted was the race track redone and I feel sure we could have races again as we did in the twenties, and what fun they were.

Prince Michael was very keen to revive the races I had enjoyed so much with the Bentley Boys who were at that time the most outstanding drivers of cars in the whole country. But there had never been a race for women until I organised one.

Prince Michael was opening the new dining-room for Brooklands and they asked me to open the Women's Rest-Room, which had always been used in the past and I gave a photograph of myself to be hung over the mantelpiece. He wrote me a very flattering letter of thanks.

The photograph was taken a long time ago by Norman Parkinson with my white Pekingese jumping off the stool in front of me.

It was only when I went down later that I realised, although it hardly showed, that there was undoubtedly fur round my shoulders. I, therefore, in the space of only two or three days, had to get another picture, in which I was not wearing fur.

Prince Michael was marvellous and made everyone feel at home. However, I thought the other speeches were too long and made mine as short as possible.

Afterwards I was photographed in exactly the same car, an M.G., as I had managed in the thirties to get round the course in – with the help of Lord De Clifford who was a racing driver. There had been no chance of my winning – I was not good enough.

The race was won by Princess Imeretinksy, who later became the fourth wife of Ernest Simpson.

When I dined with them some time later I said to him:

'I am so glad, Ernest, that you have found happiness. No one deserves it more. No one could have behaved better in the hell you passed through.'

His fingers tightened on mine until they hurt as he said very quietly:

'Thank you, Barbara, I suppose in time one will forget.'

# Chapter Six

At ninety-three I find that most of my friends are either dead or senile! I was talking to Douglas Fairbanks Junior the other day, who at eighty-three has now got married again, and he said exactly the same.

He had few friends of his own age, and those who were alive were ga-ga!

This, I am convinced, is entirely due to the modern way of not using the brain enough by reading. Douglas uses his brain because at his age he still acts a lot. Small parts – but acting! In between I know he reads and is very interested in anything that is happening at the moment.

If you ask the average person, even someone very much younger, what good book they have read lately, they say: 'Oh, well! I read the newspapers, and I watch television.'

That is the real bug-bear of the whole issue. The television is only a picture of movement and does not activate the brain in any considerable way.

What we have to remember, too, is that everything

we think, read, talk about goes into our brain, and we cannot erase it. I did not say this, it was said many years ago by a very famous parson, when he was warning of the danger of what children saw and read, because it remained in the brain for ever.

If you think about it, you will find if you dislike something or are upset by any accident or incident that has happened, you will say: 'I will not think about it again,' but you do.

If you do not use that wonderful instrument by which we live – the brain – then you become senile, and for many people this occurs at an early age.

My Mother used to say, 'Getting old is very boring, one cannot do the things one wants to do.'

The secret of why she remained so young in mind and active in body until she died at ninety-eight and a half lies in the second part of her remark: 'do the things one wants to do.'

So many people give up when they get older, giving up not only trying to be young but thinking young. When my Mother was eighty-two she said to me:

'I am learning to make lampshades at the Women's Institute. It is so interesting.'

I laughed and asked:

'But why should you want to make lampshades?'

'One never knows when it might come in useful,' she replied.

When she was older still, she had lessons in glove-making, and for many more years she was extremely interested in book-binding.

I am convinced that the most important thing is to

keep *the mind* working properly. Like many other activities of the body the more you do the more you are capable of doing and the easier it becomes.

That is why at ninety-three I have broken the World Record for twenty years running in writing twenty-three books a year – a book every fortnight.

Once we allow our brains to relax and make no effort to use them, then we age, however old we actually are in time.

When I went to Russia I found the Russians were working on the brain, and they told me that on Ginseng and B15 they have women of ninety doing a full day's work. I am sure that 'a full day's work' in Russia is exactly what it says, but it is the thought behind the exercise that counts.

In this country we do everything to slow down, depress – and what the doctors call 'calm' – the brain. This is ridiculous and very dangerous. What we should really do is accelerate the mind so that it works better, as we grow older, than it has ever worked before.

Doctors will give sleeping pills which destroy the brain – one aspirin can actually do a great deal of harm – and anyone who has a full anaesthetic over the age of fifty can lose a quarter of their brain, if not a half.

The reason that the Duchess of Windsor was completely senile before she died was due to the fact that she would keep having her face lifted when she was too old to take an anaesthetic.

Far too many men and women when they retire from their firms at sixty-five retire their brains at the same time. When, if they went on working in some form or another they would be of inestimable benefit to themselves and to the country.

I often tell the story of a very high-powered industrial tycoon who was made to retire because he had heart trouble.

He was so bored that he sat down and thought out the idea of covering haystacks with cellophane instead of having them thatched as they were at that time. He wrote to a large number of farmers with the result that his one-man business made £100,000 in its first year!

Apart from B15 we have in the National Association of Health, of which I am the Founder and President, the most marvellous ingredients now to keep one's brain young and active for ever.

One is what I call the Brain Pill, Celaton CH3 Tri-Plus, which I would not be without myself and by taking which all my Grandchildren passed their exams very highly .

Another is Co-Q-10 which we all have in our bodies but which gradually deteriorates after one is forty.

Another product which I always take myself is Lecithin, about which one of the famous American scientists said: 'No Lecithin, no brain!'

If you take these you will find that however many years you may tot up to on the calendar you will, like my Mother, retain the joy of living.

Also remember that George Bernard Shaw said: 'Youth is too good for the young.'

I sent some of my vitamins, when I heard that he was so ill, to that most lovable of comedians Arthur Askey. I had a very sweet letter from him, although he had had both legs amputated and knew he would not live very much longer. Those of you who save letters as I do will, I know, think this is one which shows the writer was not only exceedingly brave but remained cheerful until the end.

> 11 Abbots House
> St. Mary Abbots Terrace
> London

Dear Barbara,

When I received your unexpected boxes of 'Auntie Barbara's boxes of Magic Potions', I took two tablets right away – gave them a good five minutes to take effect – then rushed up to my favourite magic mirror and quoted the well-known lines – 'Mirror, mirror on the wall who is the most beautiful of them all?' and received the well-known and justified 'Barbara Cartland'.

Anyway I intend to take two more tablets today in the vain hope that I will look a little more like that lovely lady I see from time to time on TV.

You must be tired of hearing people saying 'Isn't she fantastic – how does she do it?' And I am one of them who says it. You are a wonderful and fantastic lady and your repartee should be recorded for posterity.

Meantime I will keep on with the tablets until that great day when my mirror says 'It's a tie' I will then smash it against the wall, knowing it's a liar! There will never ever be another Barbara. Or a greater admirer than

> Your old playmate
> Arthur

It was in November 1982, two days before he died, that I had the following letter.

> St Thomas' Hospital
> London SE1

Dear Barbara Cartland,

Thanks and thanks again for your nice thought and good wishes.

Needless to say, I am still in the throes of despair and still cannot fully appreciate what has happened to me. I had been pondering about retiring but now the decision has been made for me. What a lousy exit!

My only consolation is that nice people like you will give me an occasional thought. I have made many friends during the years and hope to keep them till the end of the road.

God bless and again many thanks,

> Your old playmate
> Rene
> for Arthur Askey

Besides my campaign to get everyone healthier and taking my vitamins, I am also very concerned about another problem of 'today'. Namely the present Divorce Laws.

A friend of mine went to see the best-known and most expensive divorce lawyer in London.

He began to say that his wife had left him, after twelve years of marriage, for another man. She was now demanding half the value of his house and . . .

'Do not waste our time,' the lawyer interrupted. 'You give her half of everything you possess.'

He was naturally astonished but found that what he had been told was the law. He had to sell his house which he had worked hard to own. She received £100,000 for it and £40,000 for the children.

The husband pays for their education, their holidays, their clothes and the wages of the *au pair* girl who looks after them. His wife is often difficult about his seeing them and she is now waiting until he publishes a book he has written, so that she can claim half of that.

This is just one of the dozen cases I know of personally.

The man who said that the law passed in 1976 was an 'Adulteress's Charter' was speaking the truth. It is not surprising that more and more husbands are joining the 'Divorce Law Reform Association'. Founded in 1986, it is fighting for the Rights of Men. As they say themselves:

> Divorce Law as it is put into practice is grossly unjust to husbands and their children and causes widespread and severe hardship with consequent long-term bitterness and hostility.

The monetary side of marriage was originally for the protection of the wife to ensure that she was not penniless when she grew old and unattractive, and her husband preferred a prettier and younger woman.

The pendulum has now swung violently to the benefit of the wife so that if a marriage breaks up the man can be left penniless and jobless.

A young man I knew, who was intelligent enough to form his own company, married. After a year he and his wife realised they were incompatible and had a divorce. He was forced to give his wife half his company, which meant that he could no longer carry on. He sold out to return to working for another company rather than having his own. He has sworn that he will never marry again.

It has been quoted that a leading High Court Judge returned home unexpectedly one day to find his wife in bed with two members of a famous pop group. His comments were: 'If I sue for divorce, I would lose my home and family.'

There was a recent case of a Hertfordshire dentist who had to pay his wife £250,000 as a reward for adulterous conduct.

There was also the man who was to give his half of everything, so he hired a chain-saw and literally cut all the possessions in half, including the bed, television, table, chairs, etc.

The bitterness of men who have struggled for years to establish themselves and now support a wife and her lover is understandable.

The endless tug-of-war over the children is the worst. The courts, in most cases rightly, give the custody to the wife, but women can be extraordinarily mean. Many take the money for the children from the husband and put barrier after barrier in the way of his seeing them.

One man I know rings up two or three times a week to try to speak to his daughter, whom he adores, always to be told:

'She is out!' 'Away with friends!' 'Not well!' Yet he can often hear the girl's voice in the distance.

If he goes to the courts, which is very expensive,

he will have to pay both his and his wife's fees.

A letter from the Divorce Law Reform Association to the Prime Minister brought a reply from the Political Office at 10 Downing Street. After quoting the power of the courts to give maintenance, and the adjustments that were made in 1984 it goes on:

> However, I should emphasise that these adjustments do nothing to alter the legal obligation that a husband owes to his former wife, which may continue until she remarries or dies.

It finishes:

> It is rarely possible for the two households which inevitably result from divorce to be maintained out of the available income without both parties suffering financial detriment.

In America they have marriage contracts, which if unromantic, ensure that should there be a divorce, the wife cannot claim more than agreed in the contract. In this country any contract can be overruled by the courts. This eventually leads the husband to paying, paying, and paying.

But of course the main thing is to keep families together, and that is why I am fighting for 'Wages for Mothers'.

I wanted – and still want – Parliament to pay mothers a wage to enable them to stay at home, for the first five years of a child's life.

I do not want them to have a career and leave the

child in the charge of possibly some ignorant young girl or boy who abuses it.

Remembering my success with the Prayers for Schools I sent a letter to every Member of Parliament suggesting that this might be a good idea to save the children of the future.

I received some stupid letters from some of them saying, 'Do not worry, we will give more money in the autumn.'

It was not a question of money but of having the mother with the child. One Minister actually wrote saying there was no proof that a child gets on better with its mother than any other woman.

As a mother carries her child in her body for nine months, of course the child is attached to its mother rather than to a stranger. Needless to say with such stupid answers I did not win this battle I but am still continuing to fight it.

While I was engaged in trying to make the Members of Parliament see sense, the French brought in a similar measure with great success. They paid the mother 2,000 francs for the first child, 3,000 for the second, and 4,000 for the third child, a month. After that they stopped as they did not want large families.

When Prime Minister Chirac went, they stopped the grant for the first child for no reason I could understand, but he is determined to restore it should he get back into power. The idea was also copied by Sweden, where, I have learnt, it is a great success.

It is extremely infuriating here that Members of Parliament do not understand that what children want is security and love. If they do not get it then when they grow up, especially when they come from broken homes, they are at war with the world around them.

At least Parliament had taken some notice of my fight to bring Prayers back into schools when both Houses voted for Prayers and Religious Education.

Prayers have always been terribly important to me.

I have also had extraordinary experiences which I have written down in a book called *I Seek the Miraculous*.

What I did not tell anyone for some time was that when I have finished the book I am dictating, I then say a prayer. Within twenty-four hours I have a plot for the next one.

I become more and more convinced every year that I am helped from the 'Other World', perhaps by my brother Ronald, who meant so much to me when he was alive.

The other day – it was a Thursday – for no reason I could possibly imagine, I saw him quite clearly standing near me. He was looking very young – much younger than when he died. He was smiling and I could see him for two to three seconds, absolutely as clearly as if he was in the room beside me.

Perhaps, for all I knew, something terrible was going to happen. For the moment I was nervous.

It was only on the Friday morning that I realised that it was the anniversary of Dunkirk. He had obviously come back to tell me not to worry, and that even though he had died in the War he was still alive helping me, as he had helped me when we were together.

I have enjoyed writing my non-fiction books as well as all my romantic novels. One of these was my *Book of Celebrities* (1982) which featured many of my friends, one of whom was Lady Astor.

In 1919 Lady Astor was the first woman to take her seat in the House of Commons. At first her fellow M.P.s did not take her seriously. Winston Churchill who had known her for a very long time, for example, ignored her whenever she entered the House. One day she demanded to know the reason.

He replied that he found a woman's intrusion into the House of Commons as embarrassing as if she burst into his bathroom when he had nothing to defend himself with but a sponge.

'You are not handsome enough to have worries of that kind,' she replied. Lady Astor was to become very famous for her witty repartee.

The book took me three years to write because of the difficulty in obtaining some of the unpublished photographs.

I first met Josephine Baker, who was also included, in Paris in 1925, but I did not dare to tell anyone! She was scandalising the capital with her erotic dancing and was unlike anyone I had ever seen before.

But I also discovered the other side to her character when, during World War II, she served in the Free French Air Force, fed and looked after hundreds of war orphans and adopted twelve of them.

Lord Beaverbrook the newspaper magnate once told me a sad but revealing story about himself, which I just had to include. He was a young ambitious law student who managed to get an invitation to a big dance in Newcastle, New Brunswick.

After he had hired a tail-coat, white shirt and tie he was told that he could not go because it had been discovered that he once sold newspapers on the streets.

He went home, put on the dress suit and stood in front of the mirror saying to himself:

'The day will come when they will be glad to ask me to their goddamned Assembly!'

That was the secret he had told me, and I felt that as so much time had passed I could reveal the story.

I gave this book to Prince Charles for Christmas that year because Dickie Mountbatten had written the piece about himself and I knew he would enjoy reading it. He told me afterwards that he had read it to his Grandmother. She had laughed because she had known every single person and knew every anecdote about them.

What particularly interested me was a letter from Prince Tomislav of Yugoslavia.

He had been ten when I met him first during World War II when I discovered his Mother, Queen Marie, was in a very dull, boring little house in Bedfordshire, looked after by only two servants and a very difficult lady-in-waiting.

At the time, I was looking after morale at secret stations, where they were not allowed to have any entertainment, and I managed to take her round. She was absolutely charming to everyone and they loved meeting her. At the same time they were a little disappointed she was not wearing her coronet, but thought Tomislav was a dear little boy.

As he grew older he told me that the first English girl he fell in love with was my daughter Raine.

Thirty-five years later he wrote to me about my *Book of Celebrities*, which included his Mother.

I received many letters of appreciation when I sent a copy of the book to my friends.

Their response prompted me to write another book involving friends called *Getting Older Growing Younger* in 1984. In this book I pass on many of my own well-tried recipes and experiences. Not only my own, but many from the celebrities mentioned.

I revealed that Cleopatra not only bathed in asses' milk, but improved her hair with the lotion made from a hare's foot, some date stones and the hoof of an ass!

Not many people know that Elizabeth, Empress of Austria, went to bed wearing a mask lined with veal, and Queen Alexandra hid a scar on her neck with a diamond dog-collar, and in later life wore a toupée.

Douglas Fairbanks has said to me on several occasions:

'I am blessed with more than my share of energy and I resent having to sleep at night because I cannot wait for the next day to come along.'

That was one of the comments I felt I just had to include, as I did with the comment from Zsa Zsa Gabor:

'I do not believe in a face-lift, unless it is really necessary. I never had one. Thank God for my Hungarian bone structure. A face-lift on many ladies can make them look older than they are. After all, what is wrong with wrinkles? I think they are sexy and exciting!'

What a wonderful remark from a lady who loves 'gorgeous animals, gorgeous clothes, gorgeous jewellery, gorgeous men, and gorgeous everything'.

The advice in the book, received by me from celebrities who had passed the 'first flush of youth', was invaluable to people wanting to stay young themselves.

But I could not help reminding everyone that 'nothing will age a person more than sex without love'.

To return for a moment to my novels: I have been impressed for a long time by the French, because one of the reasons they sell so many copies is because they give away presents with my books. They also believe tremendously in publicity.

For the first month of the book being published it is advertised on the television. In the second month they have it featured in all their popular magazines, with a famous actor or actress presenting it. Besides this, when you buy two copies of Barbara Cartland books you receive a present which is always original – a beautiful silk scarf which I signed 'Barbara Cartland'.

They have also given away a small mirror for one's handbag with a magnifying glass on one side, and a normal one on the other. They have had jewellery, and a number of other small presents which people appreciate because they are getting them for nothing.

I cannot get the English to understand the importance of this and therefore I do not sell so many books in England as I sell in other parts of the world.

One indication of what can happen was when Dewhursts the Butchers asked my son if they could give away one of my books when people bought £10 of their meat. We agreed, and I thought perhaps people would not think it worth spending that amount of money to get a 'Barbara Cartland'. We sold 330,000 books in that way.

When it first started I went to Dr Len Mervyn, a scientist who helps me endlessly with his expertise, and asked him how we could possibly explain that meat was part of romance.

He said to me in surprise:

'You should know already, that unless we have meat, we do not have tall, strong, handsome men.

'In fact, we have already had to reduce the height of the Army because the men are so short, and reduce the height of entrance to the Police Force twice.'

I was extremely surprised and he went on:

'It is absolutely essential for a man to have B12. Unfortunately B12 is only to be found in meat. Therefore the 'junk food' the young people eat today is not going to make them strong and handsome.'

I thought this was true, as I had already noticed when I was reviewing an old film, *The Yellow Rolls-Royce*, that every man in the film was tall.

They had already said that when they were making my films they had great trouble in finding tall men, as they did not apply to be actors.

Since then I have heard that in Japan they are determined to put at least six inches on to the Japanese, who are very small men. Therefore they are being forced, for the first time in their lives, to eat meat. They have, they told me proudly, managed to make the men eating it half-an-inch taller.

I was very excited when I began to write my five-hundredth book which I called *The Spirit of Love*.

To celebrate this a party was arranged for me at the Concordia Notte Restaurant in Bayswater organised by my friend John East who is absolutely brilliant at this sort of event.

Eighty of my friends enjoyed the special Pink Menu thought up by the owner Signor Lillo Militello. We started with fresh pink salmon followed by pasta with pink sauce, sole à la Barbara Cartland, served with pink potatoes. Then there came Strawberries Romanoff and pink liqueurs.

Guests at the top table with me were Princess Helena Moutafian, the Earl of Lichfield, Mrs Manja Leigh from Geraldo Entertainments, who organised a musical tribute to me.

Also there were H.R.H. Princess Katarina of Yugoslavia, and H.R.H. Prince Michael of Kent, who, because he had a royal appointment first, came in late for coffee. He very kindly led the singing of 'If You Were The Only Girl in the World.'

My Grandsons Viscount Lewisham and the Hon. Rupert Legge were also present, much to my delight.

Another very flattering tribute to me was when Gwen Robyns wrote my biography, *Barbara Cartland*, in what I thought was a very clever manner and it was completely and absolutely true.

In August 1983 I recommended her to the Queen Mother of Albania who was living very quietly in France with her sister. I thought it would make her happy if she had her life story told which was a very dramatic one. Almost as soon as her son was born she had to leave Albania.

She and Gwen Robyns became extremely good friends and she was grateful to me not only for introducing her to Gwen but also for the vitamins I was sending her.

For Queen Geraldine an even sadder future lay ahead. She still writes to me from her home which is now in South Africa. She lives in a small cottage on the estate owned by her son King Luka, and due to her health, is a virtual prisoner.

To turn to a lighter note for a moment, horse racing is always known to be 'The Sport of Kings' and one might say 'The Sport of Queens' albeit the Queen of Romance!

I usually write about the age when there was no other means of transport and everybody moved about with horses.

My Mother was an outstanding rider. But I regret to say that as I learnt to ride during World War I and all the good horses had gone to France with the troops, I could only ride the horses which were left behind. Therefore I did not enjoy riding as much as I should have.

However I was thrilled when the very famous racehorse owner, Ken Ivory, offered me a horse for the St. John Ambulance Brigade. It was run in my name and in my Colours, but every time it won, the money went to the St. John.

It was very generous on the part of Mr. Ivory and Amber Lance was successful at a great number of meetings. He was a magnificent looking horse and I was very proud of him. He was given a cloth bearing the St. John Emblem to wear when he was not running. He won quite a number of small races and St. John were very grateful to Mr. Ivory for making such an effort on their behalf.

Horses feature quite strongly in the first of my films, made by Gainsborough Pictures in 1987.

*A Hazard of Hearts* cost $5 million to make and was shot at Belvoir Castle belonging to the Duke of Rutland.

I have known Charles Rutland for years and he was undoubtedly one of the most handsome men I had ever seen. He was well-known for his looks and is still embarrassed when I say so. His castle is very beautiful and a perfect background for *A Hazard of Hearts* which I had written years ago in 1948.

Acting in it were many old friends including, Stewart Granger, Edward Fox, Diana Rigg, Fiona Fullerton, Helen Massey, Helena Bonham-Carter, Christopher Plummer and Marcus Gilbert.

It had the most beautiful music written for it by that wonderful composer, and a great and dear friend of mine, Laurie Johnson.

The film became Number One in the ratings when it was shown in New York. The film started at Wrotham Park which is a beautiful Georgian house, not far from Camfield and belongs to the Byng Family. However, the film really blossomed at Belvoir Castle where it had exactly the right background for the story, which is one of my favourites.

I am delighted that *A Hazard of Hearts* was shown again recently by the B.B.C. and I have received many, many letters of appreciation from excited viewers saying how much they love a story with a beginning, a middle and an end.

I have also always been delighted with the casts for the films of my books. The very beautiful Alison Doody was the heroine in *A Duel of Hearts*, with Benedict Taylor as the hero.

This film included that wonderfully handsome

actor Michael York who had also played King Charles II in my film *The Lady and the Highwayman*.

All my films are based on my books which are historical romances, and I was delighted to hear the other day of the great success of Hugh Grant.

Hugh played the hero Lucius in my film *The Lady and the Highwayman* and he also played the hero in the runaway smash hit *Four Weddings and a Funeral*.

Unfortunately three actors who also acted in my films, Stewart Granger in *A Hazard of Hearts*; Gordon Jackson (late of *Upstairs Downstairs* and *The Professionals*) and Lord Bernard Miles, who were in *The Lady and the Highwayman*, are no longer with us.

Sir John Mills is also one of the other most talented actors who has worked on my films.

I have had five films made so far, of my books, which are:

*The Flame Is Love*, which was made in America, and *A Hazard of Hearts*, *The Lady and the Highwayman*, *A Ghost in Monte Carlo* and *A Duel of Hearts*, all made by Gainsborough Films.

# *Chapter Seven*

I have interviewers coming to see me almost every day, and they are very often accompanied by photographers.

But one of the best photographs I have ever had taken of my house was taken by Derry Moore, who is now the 12th Earl of Drogheda. He took immense trouble in photographing each room. He was fascinated with the hundreds of covers from my books which decorate the secretaries' room and the corridors leading up to it.

He would be amused if he came again to find that each bathroom and, in fact, every room in the house, is stacked with books, while wall after wall is decorated with the covers of them. It is impossible not to ask: 'Where can I put the next one?'

The house certainly has a very original look about it, compared to an ordinary country house.

I got a very different view of my home Camfield Place when I flew over it, in a Tiger Moth in 1985, waving to my staff who had all come out to watch me. I had been asked if I would choose 'A Time of

My Life' for the television show with Noel Edmonds. I chose to recreate the time in 1931 when, with two R.A.F. pilots, I thought of the idea of the Aeroplane Towed Glider.

There had been gliding contests since 1923 but in 1930 new improvements had been perfected in gliders and gliding, due indirectly to the Versailles Treaty. This imposed severe restrictions on aeroplane flying in Germany but the Germans, quite undaunted, taught their pilots to fly in gliders.

These were hand-launched down a runway and once in the air, could be made to climb to great heights and remain in the air for hours.

Our idea was to attach the glider to an aeroplane, and release it when it was high enough to glide any distance required. This seemed to me to be an excellent and cheap proposition for commercial flying.

Why not a train of gliders for light commodities to be dropped off like slip coaches at various ports of call? To show the possibility of this we arranged to build a glider, tow it to ten thousand feet and let it fly over the Channel landing at a French aerodrome.

I gave the order for the glider to be started and we kept very quiet as to what we were planning. But someone talked and a month later the *Daily Mail* announced an offer of £1,000 prize to the first glider to fly the Channel both ways. We made enquiries at the *Daily Mail*'s office but they had no ideas as to how it might be done but 'just felt it might be possible'.

Gliding experts all over the country started to scheme for this prize and one of the contractors actually engaged on making my glider wanted to compete himself.

It was soon obvious that there would be a rush across the Channel on the day chosen by the *Daily Mail* for the competition to take place, and the whole thing would be turned into a 'stunt'.

Accordingly, I decided not to compete but to do something quite different.

The maker of my glider, however, was taking no chances, and by a strange coincidence it was quite impossible for the glider to be ready even twenty-four hours before the day of the race. We also had only one towing cable.

So, from Manston aerodrome on June 20th 1931 we let the Channel competitor start first, then when the released cable was dropped back to us, we attached it to the aeroplane and to the red and white 'Barbara Cartland', and turning our backs on the coast, set off across country to deliver the first aeroplane-towed glider mail.

I sat in the open aeroplane with Flying Officer Wanliss with the release hook just above my head. Flying Officer Mole was in the glider.

It was a perfect day, calm and sunny. We rose slowly, Flying Officer Wanliss being extremely anxious as it had been suggested that a weight at the back of the plane might cause it to 'turn turtle'.

We sailed smoothly across the green face of England. A cricket match was stopped to wave to us as we passed, golfers stared at us from the fairways of famous courses, the world was very beautiful and we were excited at what we were achieving.

With no mishaps we reached Reading aerodrome, a distance of about a hundred miles, where the Mayor was waiting to greet us.

When the ceremony of presenting the commemorative letter was over, the Master of Sempill, who was Vice-President of the International Commission for the Study of Motorless Flight, arrived from Heston with five aeroplanes to offer my glider the hospitality of the aerodrome.

I accepted gratefully and we flew back in style – with escort. The 'Barbara Cartland' took part in several air rallies that summer and carried a passenger from London to Blackpool, racing against the express train – being easily the winner.

The honour of being the first to cross the Channel by glider actually belonged to Lissart Beardmore, a Canadian, who crossed the day before the *Daily Mail* competition which was won by a German.

'I think a new epoch in air travel has begun,' Herr Kronfield, the winner, said.

But the Air Ministry thought otherwise and stopped aeroplane-towing as being too dangerous. Gliders in England then returned to hand-launching, but Germany did not forget what had been proved by the experiment and they used the gliders in the invasion of Crete. We, the British, did not use them until 'D Day'.

The 'Barbara Cartland', after being hand-launched, set up a record for British gliders with a falling flight of four and three-quarter miles. But on landing from a second flight she was blown over three times. The pilot escaped injury but what remained of the 'Barbara Cartland' was taken to the scrapheap.

The sequel to this is that in 1984 I received at Kennedy Airport, America's Bishop Wright Air

Industry Award for my contribution to the development of aviation. From the British I did not even get so much as a postcard.

The fact that no one had thought of the glider for the television programme in 1985 before caused a great deal of excitement.

Therefore at Hatfield Aerodrome which is near my house I arranged to have the 'Barbara Cartland glider' redone exactly as it had been before. They actually took the same Tiger Moth out of the museum where it was situated to tow the glider.

At the last moment, just as I was ready to step into the aeroplane, to release the glider so that it floated down to the ground, the Air Ministry said I was not allowed to fly. I asked why not and the officer in charge said: 'If Barbara Cartland is killed it would be the same as smashing Concorde.'

This meant that someone else would have to be found to take my place.

The girl who took my place said, rather sourly I thought:

'No one cares about me!'

She got into the Tiger Moth and flew across the aerodrome, being photographed for the television programme. When she returned I thanked her profusely for risking her life on my behalf.

My staff at Camfield Place were more than mere onlookers when, in March 1992, they became very involved in the country's General Election.

I was very worried about it, as the nightly polls showed that the Conservatives were far behind the Labour.

When I was in London one of the advisers in the

House of Commons asked me to meet him at the Dorchester. He told me they were very worried and, in fact, they had had a meeting to decide who they should put forward as their next Prime Minister, if they failed under John Major, as they were expecting a Hung Parliament.

I understood what they were feeling because I had seen the polls myself on the television every night. There was no doubt that Labour were ahead and the Conservatives were doing very badly.

I said to them:

'We have not lost yet!'

I went back home and said to my chief secretary Mrs. Clark:

'This is terrible! We must do something!'

She said: 'Of course we must!'

We both sat thinking what we could do.

Finally I dictated to her a letter which she took down in shorthand.

Sir,

I am very surprised that the Church has not, in any way, pointed out to the people that Mr. Kinnock is an avowed atheist, and his wife said the other day:

'I do not believe in God, and when I get to No. 10 I am going on teaching children.'

If you vote for Kinnock, you are voting against Christ who said: 'Suffer little children to come unto me.'

Yours
Barbara Cartland

We sent this letter to 967 newspapers and magazines. We received hundreds of letters back, most of them saying that they had no idea, although they had always voted Labour in the past, that Mr. Kinnock was an atheist.

It did not win the Election, but I am convinced that it is due to my letters that the Conservative votes soared up and we had a far bigger majority than was expected.

I am horrified that not a word was said by the Archbishop of Canterbury or any Member of the Church, against Mr. Kinnock who is an avowed atheist.

Because so many of the letters were very decisive, I sent the strongest twenty to the Archbishop of Canterbury who had not helped in any way with my campaign to bring the Prayers back into the schools.

After almost a month he replied through one of the Bishops saying that he thought Mr. and Mrs. Kinnock's religion was their private affair.

By law that is not true. If someone stands to represent you or me, we are entitled to know what he or she believes in before we accept them as our Leader.

Following the Conservative win, I received a wonderful letter from John Major, thanking me for my invaluable support.

I could not have done all this, of course, without help. I have been very fortunate in having a wonderful staff of people who help me in every possible way.

My Chief Secretary, Hazel Clark, has been with me for twenty years and has done five hundred books. She is a natural organiser and has also got a memory like an *Encyclopaedia Britannica*. She not only arranges everything, but also copes with the enormous number of letters – about 32,000 a year – from all over the world, from people asking what they should eat and what they should do to keep young and healthy.

My Chef, Nigel Gordon, who has been with me for twenty-seven years, has helped me write five cookery books. He is a Scot and a marvellous inventor of new dishes, so we never eat the same day after day.

My Housekeeper, Mrs. Robinson, who is nearly eighty, is very capable, and has been with me for forty-five years.

My Head Gardener, Les Oakes, has been here thirty-five years.

My one extravagance is that I have a hairdresser every day of the year.

Mrs. Austen is a very great friend, who has been with me for thirty years and she has been all over the world with me. She is a great success in every country we visit.

She is absolutely marvellous with hair and takes a great interest in turning me out so that I am a credit to her.

I have a charming Secretary now, Mrs. Smith, who has helped me for five years. She is brilliant at shorthand and the best person I have ever had to dictate to, as she never makes a sound, and therefore does not interrupt me.

I realise how lucky I am to have all these people who feel they are part of the Show and who help me in every possible way they can.

We all need supportive friends.

A friend of mine who has done marvels for the children suffering in Romania which has given me many sleepless nights is a lady called Judy Almond.

She is the wife of a local doctor and she has raised many thousands of pounds on her own locally. She has gone three times to Romania to help the children who are suffering not only from every sort of disease from which they are unlikely to recover but also have no comforts whatsoever.

She has taken with her nappies, vitamins and everything she could possibly get locally. She has done the most amazing work in a country which is still sadly in need of sympathy from us.

She came into my life when I arrived at Camfield and found that I had, as I have already said, the Magic Tree in the garden planted by Elizabeth I, when she was a prisoner at Hatfield House.

Judy had the acorns made into pendants and also showed me how to put the leaves into a small compact which could be included in anyone's purse. She was, however, known as a White Witch because when she was a little girl in Canada, the White Witch there was dying and she said to Judy, 'I am going to give you my powers.'

Very bravely Judy said she did not want them. However, the Witch insisted as it would help so many people and make them happy.

Judy has certainly done that when she has spent her life telling people how to help others and has now succeeded in helping so many children in Romania.

She blesses the leaves I have taken from my tree

which I know are very lucky. I wear an acorn round my neck together with a cross which has been blessed by a priest. Also my sons have an acorn each which they carry in their pockets.

So many people have told me they had found their greatest desire after they had received something from the Tree which had had Judy's blessing.

There was a family in Scotland who for fifteen years had wanted a baby but failed to have one. They came to me for help and I said you must take my vitamins and the wife must wear one of my lucky charms from the tree in my garden. Their first baby was a daughter who was extremely pretty and became the champion baby of Sutherland. No one could have done better.

I am also a great believer in ginseng. Ortis of Belgium gave me as a present a large bottle of their ginseng for every guest at my ninetieth birthday party. This was because I had said over and over again that ginseng is the oldest drink in the world going back to 1 BC made from the special root grown in China.

It was first introduced to us by the Secretary of State for America, Henry Kissinger. He was over fifty and flew all over Europe and did not suffer in any way from jet-lag. This was due to the fact that he was taking ginseng.

It was only the other day when I was writing about this that I discovered that the United States brought in a law in which you could not go to the moon or even try to get there if you did not take ginseng, simply because it has such a good effect on you.

I personally take a small amount of Ortis's Special

Ginseng every morning and find it gives me energy to work during the day and also to enjoy myself.

One other drink which is very important is Norfolk Punch. I was absolutely thrilled to discover that it was so good. I realised the reason it is so marvellous is because Norfolk is the only county in England that has so much Selenium in the soil.

I looked through various records and found they had practically no cancer, very little heart problems, and great virility.

It was then I looked into Selenium over the world and discovered the Americans were saying it cured breast cancer.

I am always very wary in saying anything is a complete cure because every person is different just as every country is different. But there is no doubt at all that Norfolk Punch is a wonderful pick-me-up for people who are ill. It certainly takes away asthma as the past Bishop of Southwark, the Right Reverend Mervyn Stockwood, will testify.

I myself take it every night before I go to bed. I find it makes me sleep well and I am quite certain that it is due to Norfolk Punch combined with Flame, about which I will write later, that I have been able to break the world record of the number of books I have written.

Norfolk Punch has also been introduced into Australia by the Barbara Cartland House in Perth, which is all pink, owned by Pamela Pagano and her husband. They have painted everything pink, including the outside of the house, and Norfolk Punch is one of the best English products they have for sale.

I am always delighted to introduce something new to the country. At the beginning of 1984 I decided to introduce to England the first *nouvelle cuisine* cookery book as one had not been published before.

The difficulty was that my own chef, Nigel Gordon, who had never seen *nouvelle cuisine* nor had the woman chef whom the publishers sent down to help. The photographer was completely ignorant on the matter and it was therefore up to me to make them understand exactly what *nouvelle cuisine* meant in France.

Now of course we are all used to it but at the time no one had any idea it was different from any other cooking. I had to go down to the kitchen early in the morning and start them off cooking something. Then I would find they had put on too much sauce for the pictures and for the French idea of *nouvelle cuisine*.

'Throw it away,' I would say, 'and start again.'

Very good-temperedly they did. Personally I would have thrown the saucepan at me.

Eventually, however, we produced a delightful book called *The Romance of Food* which afterwards was used by the House of Commons in the hope of making them more romantic!

It was very hot when we were making the food and they had to put Polyfilla in some of the cream as it was melting before the photographs could be taken.

The publishers were entranced with the ornaments I put into the pictures to complement the superb food, which was unquestionably French.

It is always said that 'a way to a man's heart is through his stomach' so what better way did I have for Valentine's Day 1984 than to bring out my book?

It had a delightful pink cover and made the food seem to be a work of art on the plate. The recipes were delicious and designed to stimulate the palate. They had such wonderful names as 'Flower of the Heart' and 'The Duc's Fantasy'.

Christina Foyle was kind enough to give me a Foyle's Luncheon for the book, and the Chairman on that occasion was Mr. Charles Irving, the Member of Parliament who was instrumental in bringing it to the House.

Obviously a large number of my recipes came from France, as it is a country I visit frequently.

In October 1984 I went to Paris to be on the Television Show *Champs-Elysées* which has an audience of sixteen million people. The whole interview was brilliantly done. I arrived on the set in a horse-drawn carriage and although I spoke in English there was a translator speaking French overhead.

Unfortunately I am not very good at French but I ended the show with the words, *'Je t'adore Paris. Paris est la plus belle cité de tout le monde. Merci bien! Bonne chance!'*

There were at least 500 people present, and after the show they were all given a glass of champagne.

It was in 1988 that I went to Paris to receive the highest Award, the Gold Medal of Paris, from the Mayor, Monsieur Chirac for my contribution to literature which has resulted in a lot of employment. At that time I had sold 25,000,000 books in France.

We had a very moving party at the Mairie. They provided champagne and delicious food for the guests. I could not help thinking it was something I would not get at Buckingham Palace.

In the evening my French publishers paid for an hour's television show. There were questions and an interview which was filmed, after which I was taken outside to the park in a white Rolls-Royce, by permission of the Prime Minister, to watch the most wonderful fireworks. There was 'B.C.' in stars and bursts of pink roses. It is the first time such a tribute has been given to an author.

In 1991, I managed to achieve something which was very necessary for the whole country.

In six years I had only been able to get one award – an M.B.E. – for Hertfordshire, and the man died two months after receiving it.

It seemed impossible for any ordinary person to receive an award, however much he had done for this country, until he was on the way to the graveyard. But what was so unfair was that civil servants, good, bad or indifferent, received an automatic award, and so did Members of Parliament. If they enter Parliament at the age of twenty-five when they were forty-five they are made a peer, regardless of what they have done in the meantime.

I did not say to John Major that I personally had been put forward seven times to my knowledge, but I did tell him how unfair I thought the system was.

The Prime Minister listened attentively to my views on awards and said that he would see to it. Later the following year he brought in the ruling that in future awards should be given for 'Merit' which is what I think is completely fair.

In 1991, however, I had received my award,

because when a certain person, whom I am not allowed to name, was asked if I should have it, they said:

'As Barbara is nearing retiring age, I think she should have it!' I was nearly ninety!

It was very well arranged.

The Lord Chamberlain wrote to me and said that when I arrived with my two sons – I had notified them that they were coming with me – they were to hand in his letter, which they did and were taken in by a different door from me.

I was taken up a very familiar staircase which has no railings, which I had climbed many times before.

I was shown into a large Drawing Room, where there were sixteen men waiting.

I was the only woman!

I was told that they were the Lord Lieutenants of various counties.

They were there to learn how to kneel in front of the Queen when she placed the sword on their shoulders to make them Knights.

But when they rehearsed, several of them fell off the stool. The Lord Lieutenant from one county said:

'I cannot see, I cannot hear and I cannot kneel.'

Then we went down to the Music Room where the Band was playing and the Queen had already arrived with her Guard of Honour, the Beefeaters.

I was the second person to be awarded and the Queen had a little difficulty pinning it on my coat.

When I turned round I found there were about three hundred other people in the room of all ages. These, of course, were the civil servants whom I had complained had an award automatically.

The sixteen men from upstairs looked very tired and old when they took their seats, which demonstrated to me more strongly than ever, how unfair the arrangements were.

When the Queen left with her bodyguard, the Steward then asked me if I would follow her. When I got outside I was given the beautiful medal and the diamond brooch which is exactly what a man receives when he becomes a Knight.

The man giving it then said:

'Do you want to go down in the lift?'

I had no idea there was a lift in Buckingham Palace and I feel sure it has only been put in recently for the Queen Mother.

However, I said I would have liked to come up in the lift, but was determined to walk down as my sons, who had joined me, would see more of the Palace if we did so.

We walked down through several places where there were magnificent pictures which I had seen before but of course they had not. We then went outside to where the Press were waiting to take photographs of those who had received an award. Following the announcement I received many hundreds of telegrams and letters of congratulations from fans all over the world.

I cannot conclude my book without telling you about the 'Miracle' which has happened to me, which I consider to be one of the most exciting discoveries ever made in the Health Movement.

I woke up one night in 1992 unable to breathe.

I aroused my son who was sleeping in the next

room and told him what had happened. He gave me some brandy and said that I must see a doctor.

As I could not think of anything in the Health Movement which would help me, I sent for one. I was very reluctant, as doctors' medicines always have a side effect.

The doctor told me I had too much water around my heart, and it had been leaking into my lung, which was why I could not speak.

I took the pills the doctor gave me.

My legs started to feel rather painful, but I felt that it must be old age!

Quite by chance a month later my son was taking some of my vitamins back to London, and he took with him one of the diuretics the doctor had given me.

Glen rang the next day to tell me that it was very dangerous because it had affected his legs, and that he could hardly walk to the Tube station! This made me realise why my legs had been feeling so painful.

I went, at once, to see Michael Van Straten, an old friend, who is our most brilliant osteopath. He was horrified because all the strength behind my knees had gone.

He told me to take fresh nettle tea for my heart which has been most effective. For my legs he gave me Acupuncture and had them massaged.

Then he said he had some pills which would help me, which had come to him from Keith Pollitt, owner of a leading health company. He told me they would be good for my bones and that I was to take four a day. Of course being me, I took eight a day to make quite certain!

I felt so much better, and I was very pleased with the pills.

Keith Pollitt has that other wonderful health product called Bio-strath, which I had brought into the country twenty-seven years ago.

Because the Health pills came from him, I thought they must be good so I kept on taking them.

A few weeks later I was with the wonderful Joseph Corvo, whose 'Zone Therapy' works on the veins. I told him about my heart and as he is also a healer, he put his hand on it and prayed.

Suddenly he said:

'It is a miracle!'

He was looking at my bare arms. He went on:

'You are ninety-one but your arms are the soft, white arms of a girl of eighteen, and where are your lines?'

I had always had them between my shoulder and my elbow, and now they had all gone.

When I returned home I looked at my body, and found it was the same – very white and without a single line of any sort. In fact, it was exactly as it was when I was young.

I got in touch with Keith Pollitt and told him what had happened. He was astonished! He knew his product contained the best calcium but this had never happened before.

Joseph Corvo has explained the importance of this in his new book entitled *Backache Cure*. He says that we all have calcium in our bodies, especially in our bones. It is very important as we get older and use up a lot of calcium that it is put back.

No doctor has ever told me this.

Calcium pours out of a woman when she has children, especially if she breast feeds them, when she has a period or the menopause. It is essential that it is replaced by the correct calcium which is combined with Boron and Vitamin D. If those are missing the calcium does not go into the bones.

When people get old, men especially, their heads bend forward and they get Osteoporosis. This is because their bones are crumbling for lack of calcium.

Everybody will think that I should have known I needed calcium for my bones, but this was really the first time I had been told to take it.

The pills I am taking now do not only work inside so that I feel very much younger, but this extraordinary alteration to the outside of my body has never occurred before.

The first thing I said to Keith Pollitt was that we must have a 'Face Cream'.

I have been using the pills for my body for about two and half months, but I only received the Face Cream three weeks later. Since then people have been telling me how well I look, and also how I look much younger. I gave the Face Cream to one of my Secretaries who is fifty-four. She had deep lines on her long neck. In a week the lines on her neck had gone completely.

This is all very exciting as it means that one can go on looking pretty until one is very, very old.

As it is something quite new we had to think of a name for it. Keith Pollitt, who is romantic, found a goddess called Ayesha who, when she grew old, walked through a 'Blue Flame'. She was then rejuvenated so that she lived, young and beautiful, for ever.

I wanted it to be called 'Beauty for Ever', but unfortunately the Powers That Be refused to allow us to do that, so it is called 'Flame' because it is easy to remember.

It is very, very exciting because here we have a product that not only restores our bones, so that we do not have Osteoporosis, but we can look beautiful at the same time. I promise you that what it has done for me is really fantastic.

I am extremely grateful to Keith Pollitt for having discovered it first, very grateful to Michael Van Straten for having suggested it, and to Joseph Corvo for seeing what I would not have noticed.

I do think it is thrilling for us all. We must be grateful to these three brilliant men.

One more extraordinary thing happened.

Mrs. Newman, who is the wife of Archie Newman, who you will remember arranged for me to sing with the Royal Philharmonic Orchestra, rang me up to say she knew I would be sorry to hear that her husband was dying.

Through bad teeth his body was poisoned. Unfortunately the doctors were unable to help him any more.

As he was so fond of me, she thought I would like to speak to him, as it would make him happy.

I rang St. Mary's Hospital and got straight through to him and said:

'I love you, Archie. But you must make an effort not to leave us. We cannot do without you and your marvellous music!'

He was just strong enough to say:

'I ... love ... you ... Barbara! I ... love ... you ... Barbara!'

I rang him up the next morning, and in the evening, and the same thing happened.

I suddenly had an idea, and I said to his wife:

'Look, try him with Flame. It might help him, or it might not. At the same time, it has such wonderful properties that I feel it is worth a chance.'

I also asked my friend, Graham Wyley, the healer who had cured so many of my friends to help.

Archie's wife agreed that he should try the Flame and I said:

'I should not tell the doctors, because they are certain to say it is hopeless.'

She crushed one up, gave it to him and he took it because I had suggested it.

The next morning he sat in bed, to everyone's entire astonishment, asked for his glasses and wrote two letters. The same thing happened the next day and they had, what was to them, a very happy Easter.

Then I rang again on Easter Monday and there was no answer from the hospital, so I rang Mrs. Newman. She said that Archie had been marvellous just over Easter, and then he had slipped away peacefully in his sleep.

It was wonderful. But at the same time I could not help feeling that because he was only sixty-three that if we had started earlier, especially with the help of Graham Wyley, we would have saved his life.

Flame comes from Denmark and I was invited there with my son, to go on their big and most exciting television show where I was interviewed by the most handsome Jarl Friis Mikkelsen.

He was very clever and thought of something that I had never experienced before. There was a most beautiful set all coloured pink, and when my son entered wearing the kilt, he did so to the music and a film of the Scots Guards.

There was a lovely audience of a great number of people and the programme was going out the next day on television over the whole country.

He asked me to end the show with a prayer and I recited one that I had written myself:

One thing I know, life can never die,
    Translucent, splendid flaming like the sun.
Only our bodies wither and deny
    The Life Force when our strength is done.

Let us transmit this wonderful fire,
    Its force and power from God above
And know eternally it is His
    In every act of Love.

I have asked for this prayer to be said at my funeral.

I would now like to express to you my beliefs.

We all want to find the World behind the World, we all want to step through the Looking Glass, we all want the security of knowing we are not alone and that death is not the end. It is so easy to say you must have faith but difficult to be sure.

What I do believe, as I have said in my poem, is that you cannot have death in life – that is impossible – and life is eternal. Only our bodies, like every-thing else in nature, when they are old, decay and are thrown away, but the Life-Force within us remains.

What I believe and which has been proved so often in the East, is that in the Wheel of Rebirth we come back with all our good qualities and also our debts to humanity.

There is no other explanation as to why Mozart could play the violin perfectly at the age of four and why a little girl, aged three, can play chess with the great experts.

There are numerable examples of this not only in the past but appearing every day in the newspapers and it would be an unbelievable waste if the brilliant brain of someone like Winston Churchill were just lost because we believed he had died.

As Kipling put it so clearly:

> They will come back, come back again
> As long as the red earth rolls,
> God never wasted a leaf or tree,
> Do you think He would squander souls?

During every war people consult clairvoyants, astrologers and palmists but I have proved from long experience that though sometimes they are right, they are very often wrong which causes a great deal of unnecessary suffering.

What is important for all of us, is that we should try and reach the Divine within ourselves and actu-ally this is perfectly possible for everyone. We can do this through Concentration, Meditation, Positive

Thinking or what has been called for thousands of years – Prayer.

Prayer is not just a begging bowl for our needs, but something far more esoteric and wonderful. It is an uplifting of the heart and spirit and it happens not at specified times that we choose, but a hundred times a day often without our being consciously aware of it.

Every time we feel that quick uplift within us at the sight of beauty, the sound of music or the note of love in someone's voice, that is Prayer and our link with the world beyond this.

Sunshine on still water, the breeze in the trees, leafless branches against a winter's sky and in the passing of the second I feel with them and that is a Prayer.

In the ecstasy that happens between a man and a woman when they really love each other and they 'make love', that is the nearest we get in this dimension to the Love of God or the Life-Force, whichever you like to call it.

It is available for everyone and we just have to have the initiative and the commonsense to lift ourselves towards the Infinite.

God Bless You All. And remember what I have said so often:

IF YOU WANT LOVE YOU HAVE TO *GIVE* LOVE

# *Index*